The Working Reader

The Working Reader

Mary Lou Conlin
Cuyahoga Community College

Houghton Mifflin Company   Boston   New York

Senior Sponsoring Editor: Mary Jo Southern
Editorial Development: Bruce Cantley
Senior Project Editor: Fred Burns
Senior Production/Design Coordinator: Jill Haber
Senior Manufacturing Manager: Sally Culler
Senior Marketing Manager: Nancy Lyman

Cover credit:
GARDE SIGNS, 1926
Paul Klee, 1879–1940, Swiss
Barnes Foundation, Marion, Pennsylvania

Acknowledgments for reprinted materials begin on page 215.

Printed in the U.S.A.

Library of Congress Catalog Card Number: 99–71992

ISBN: 0-395-92920-2

123456789-BBS-04-03-02-01-00

Contents

Preface

The purpose of *The Working Reader* is to provide students with a variety of readings that relate to the working world and to work-related issues. Beginning with readings that provide differing views of and attitudes toward "work," the readings continue thematically through decisions students face in choosing a career and balancing work and family to readings related to workplace issues: ethics, time management, problem solving, decision making, discrimination, harassment, and technology. *The Working Reader* concludes with readings related to lifelong learning, changing careers, and retirement.

The questions and assignments related to the readings address the foundation skills of reading, writing, thinking critically, and other competencies needed for success in both the academic and working worlds. Through the Questions About the Readings, students are asked to determine main ideas and significant details, interpret graphs and tables, and evaluate the accuracy of the information in the various readings. Through the Thinking Critically questions, students can develop their creative thinking, decision-making, problem-solving, and reasoning skills. Instructors may choose to have students answer the reading and thinking critically questions either in class discussions, which provide an opportunity to evaluate their speaking skills, or in writing. Through the Writing Assignments, students are asked to communicate their ideas and information in essays, summaries, reports, letters, tables, and other composition forms they will use academically and in their future work.

The Working Reader also addresses many of the skills and competencies defined under the goals of America 2000 and Goals 2000. Developed in response to complaints of parents, employers, and others that students graduate from high school—even from college—without the necessary skills and competencies to succeed in a working world that is no longer based on agriculture or manufacturing but on technology, President George Bush and the nation's governors agreed to the following six national goals in education to be achieved by the year 2000, titled America 2000:

Goal 1:   Readiness for School
                            By the year 2000, all children in America will
                                start school ready to learn.

Goal 2:   High School Completion
                            By the year 2000, the high school graduation
                                rate will increase to at least 90 percent.

Goal 3:   Student Achievement and Citizenship
                            By the year 2000, American students will
                                leave grades four, eight, and twelve hav-
                                ing demonstrated competency in challeng-
                                ing subject matter including English,
                                mathematics, science, history, and geog-
                                raphy; and every school in America will
                                ensure that all students learn to use their
                                minds well, so they may be prepared for
                                responsible citizenship, further learning,
                                and productive employment in our mod-
                                ern economy.

Goal 4:   Science and Mathematics
                            By the year 2000, U.S. students will be first
                                in the world in science and mathematics
                                achievement.

Goal 5:   Adult Literacy and Lifelong Learning
                            By the year 2000, every adult American will
                                be literate and will possess the knowledge
                                and skills necessary to compete in a glo-
                                bal economy and exercise the rights and
                                responsibilities of citizenship.

Goal 6:   Safe, Disciplined, and Drug-Free Schools
                            By the year 2000, every school in America
                                will be free of drugs and violence and will
                                offer a disciplined environment conducive
                                to learning.

The goals, with two additional ones related to programs for teachers and
increasing parental involvement in the schools, became Goals 2000 and
the basis for the National Education Act, passed by Congress in January
1994.

In May 1990, in response to the America 2000 education strategy and,
more specifically, to Goal 5 and its objectives, the Secretary's Commis-

sion on Achieving Necessary Skills (SCANS) was established by then Secretary of Labor Elizabeth Dole. The Commission—made up of representatives from business, industry, labor, education, government, and research organizations—was directed to advise the secretary on the level of skills required to enter employment and to

- define the skills needed for employment
- propose acceptable levels of proficiency
- suggest effective ways to assess proficiency, and
- develop a dissemination strategy for the nation's schools, businesses, and homes.

The Commission published its initial report, *What Work Requires of Schools: A SCANS Report for America 2000,* in June 1991. The report defined the following three-part foundation of basic skills, thinking skills, and personal qualities, and five competencies required for solid job performance.

A Three-Part Foundation

Basic Skills: Reads, writes, performs arithmetic and mathematical operations, listens, and speaks

A. *Reading*—locates, understands, and interprets written information in prose and in documents such as manuals, graphs, and schedules
B. *Writing*—communicates thoughts, ideas, information, and messages in writing; and creates documents such as letters, directions, manuals, reports, graphs, and flow charts
C. *Arithmetic/Mathematics*—performs basic computations and approaches practical problems by choosing appropriately from a variety of mathematical techniques
D. *Listening*—receives, attends to, interprets, and responds to verbal messages and other cues
E. *Speaking*—organizes ideas and communicates orally

Thinking Skills: Thinks creatively, makes decisions, solves problems, visualizes, knows how to learn, and reasons

A. *Creative Thinking*—generates new ideas
B. *Decision Making*—specifies goals and constraints, generates alternatives, considers risks, and evaluates and chooses best alternative
C. *Problem Solving*—recognizes problems and devises and implements plan of action
D. *Seeing Things in the Mind's Eye*—organizes, and processes symbols, pictures, graphs, objects, and other information

E. *Knowing How to Learn*—uses efficient learning techniques to acquire and apply new knowledge and skills

F. *Reasoning*—discovers a rule or principle underlying the relationship between two or more objects and applies it when solving a problem

Personal Qualities: Displays responsibility, self-esteem, sociability, self-management, and integrity and honesty

A. *Responsibility*—exerts a high level of effort and perseveres towards goal attainment

B. *Self-Esteem*—believes in own self-worth and maintains a positive view of self

C. *Sociability*—demonstrates understanding, friendliness, adaptability, empathy, and politeness in group settings

D. *Self-Management*—assesses self accurately, sets personal goals, monitors progress, and exhibits self-control

E. *Integrity/Honesty*—chooses ethical courses of action

Five Competencies

Resources: Identifies, organizes, plans, and allocates resources

A. *Time*—Selects goal-relevant activities, ranks them, allocates time, and prepares and follows schedules

B. *Money*—Uses or prepares budgets, makes forecasts, keeps records, and makes adjustments to meet objectives

C. *Material and Facilities*—Acquires, stores, allocates, and uses materials or space efficiently

D. *Human Resources*—Assesses skills and distributes work accordingly, evaluates performance and provides feedback

Interpersonal: Works with others

A. *Participates as Member of a Team*—contributes to group effort

B. *Teaches Others New Skills*

C. *Serves Clients/Customers*—works to satisfy customers' expectations

D. *Exercises Leadership*—communicates ideas to justify position, persuades and convinces others, responsibly challenges existing procedures and policies

E. *Negotiates*—works toward agreements involving exchange of resources, resolves divergent interests

F. *Works with Diversity*—works well with men and women from diverse backgrounds

Information: Acquires and uses information

A. *Acquires and Evaluates Information*
B. *Organizes and Maintains Information*
C. *Interprets and Communicates Information*
D. *Uses Computers to Process Information*

Systems: Understands complex inter-relationships

A. *Understands Systems*—knows how social, organizational, and technological systems work and operates effectively with them
B. *Monitors and Corrects Performance*—distinguishes trends, predicts im-
   pacts on system operations, diagnoses deviations in systems' performance and corrects malfunctions
C. *Improves or Designs Systems*—suggests modifications to existing systems and develops new or alternative systems to improve performance

Technology: Works with a variety of technologies

A. *Selects Technology*—chooses procedures, tools or equipment including
   computers and related technologies
B. *Applies Technology to Task*—Understands overall intent and proper procedures for setup and operation of equipment
C. *Maintains and Troubleshoots Equipment*—Prevents, identifies, or solves
   problems with equipment, including computers and other technologies

The SCANS skills and competencies are widely supported in the working world. Through the reading selections and their questions and assignments, *The Working Reader* concentrates, primarily, on the foundation
skills but also addresses many of the competencies and proposes thereby
to improve the student's preparation for and successful transition from
school to the working world.

Apparatus

Each reading selection in the chapters that follow is preceded by the following study helps:

- Headnotes provide information about the author and context of
  the selection to help students understand and enjoy the selection.
- Before You Read questions help students think critically about the
  topic of the selection and about their own thoughts related to the
  topic.
- Words to Know lists define unfamiliar words and clarify allusions
  that might be unfamiliar or regional.

- Exercises promote comprehension, critical thinking, and development of the foundation skills and competencies.
  - Questions About the Reading are designed to help students locate, understand, and interpret the selection's meaning, whether stated or implied.
  - Thinking Critically questions ask students to analyze and react to the selection's ideas and to relate the ideas to their own lives and the SCANS skills and competencies
  - Writing Assignments are related to the topic of the selection and are designed to encourage students to generate ideas and develop them into a variety of written forms: journal entries, essays, summaries, reports, letters, and résumés and such visual aids as tables, pie charts, and graphs.

Support for Instructors

The Instructor's Manual for *The Working Reader* offers instructors the following supplemental materials:

- Two model syllabi
- Suggested answers to the reading and thinking critically questions
- Chapter quizzes

Acknowledgments

I wish to think the following reviewers who have provided valuable comments related to the early draft of the text: Bob Akin, Houston Community College; Beverly A. Butler, Shippensburg University; Sandra Carey, Lexington Community College; Jayne Decker, University of Maine at Farmington; Robert M. Esch, University of Texas at El Paso; Ghazala F. Hashmi, Averett College; Jeannine W. Morgan, St. John's River Community College; Carolyn Russell, Rio Hondo College; Robert Scattergood, Belmont Technical College, Emeritus; Elizabeth Slifer, College of Southern Idaho; Linda Suddeth Smith, Midlands Technical College; Deborah Weaver Parker, Albuquerque TVI Community College; Linda S. Weeks, Dyersburg State Community College.

I especially want to thank the many people I have worked with at Houghton Mifflin Company over more than twenty years of producing twenty-some texts in varying editions. Beginning with Nader Dareshori, Dean Johnson, and Mark Mahan for the first texts in 1978 and continuing with Mary Jo Southern, Jennifer Roderick, and Bruce Cantley for this and other recent texts, no one could ask for a better, more inspiring, and supportive relationship.

To the Student

The Working Reader provides you with a series of reading selections that relate to choosing your future work, to the place of work in your life, and to concerns you will face related to your work and your personal life. Based on the readings and your responses to the questions and assignments related to the readings, you will develop the reading, writing, and thinking skills you need to succeed in your academic and working careers. These are skills, known as the SCANS foundation skills, that have been defined by academic, business, and industry professionals as essential for success in the working world. You will find the skills listed inside the covers of this book and also in the preface.

Through the Questions About the Reading, you will be asked to determine main ideas and significant details, interpret graphs and tables, and evaluate the accuracy of the information in the various reading selections. Through the Thinking Critically questions and your responses to them in speech or in writing, you will develop your creative thinking, decision-making, problem-solving, and reasoning skills. Through the Writing Assignments, you will be asked to communicate your ideas and information in essays, reports, letters, charts, and other composition forms. You will demonstrate your personal qualities, such as responsibility and ability to work with others, by such things as completing your assigned course work and collaborating with classmates on assignments. These qualities are known as the SCANS competencies. The competencies are listed inside the covers of this book and in the preface.

Although some of the SCANS competencies can be carried out only "on-the-job," the assignments provide opportunities for you to demonstrate your ability to allocate resources, such as your time; you interpersonal competency by working with others on assignments; your competency in handling information and understanding systems through the writing assignments; and your understanding of technology by utilizing the computer in research and other assignments.

By joining the skills and competencies required in your academic work with those needed in the working world, as this book attempts to do, you will come to appreciate their relationship and improve your success in both careers.

The Working Reader

1

Work—What Is It?

WHEN PEOPLE FIRST meet, they generally ask each other, "What do you do?" While the kind of work a person does can establish a common interest or something to talk about, we tend to judge, even classify, people by the work they do. In "What You Do Is What You Are," Nickie McWhirter questions whether work is a valid basis for determining the status or worth of a person.

But what is *work*? To some people, digging in a garden is a pleasure and does not seem like work; to other people, gardening is hard, unpleasant toil. In his essay "Work and Play," Robert Murray Davis shows us the difference between his view and that of his father about what constitutes work. And in "My Mother Never Worked," Bonnie Smith-Yackel wants us to question still another view of what we call work.

The fact is, your work may be the activity by which you identify your principal role in life. But will you think of your work as a hateful necessity to make money or as enjoyment and self-fulfillment? In "Working Just to Live Is Perverted into Living Just to Work," Ana Veciana-Suarez questions whether our work should be allowed to take over our lives.

Hopefully, you will choose a satisfying career—whether it's your first or a later choice. Hopefully, too, whatever work you choose, you will be able to balance your work and your personal life.

In this chapter, you will be asked to begin keeping a journal in addition to answering the questions related to understanding and thinking critically about the reading selections. You will also write an essay and a summary. As you proceed through the text, you will see how these traditional academic composition forms relate to the writing that is required in the working world, such as a report and an abstract or an executive summary. The requirements for the journal, essay, and summary assignments follow.

The Journal

A journal is a written record of events, thoughts, reminders, or ideas. Your instructor may suggest that your initial journal entries be freewriting or brainstorming. Freewriting is simply writing down whatever comes to mind. The purpose of freewriting is to get you started writing and to generate ideas for an essay or other composition or even a speech.

Suppose your instructor asks you to think about the kind of work you want to do. Your freewriting might look like this:

> I like physical activity. Not good at sitting still. Like sports. Good at sports. Want to work with people and kids.

Now suppose you are asked to write an essay about the kind of work you may want to do and to explain the training you think you would need for that kind of work. Your freewriting indicated that you like and are good at sports. You may want to brainstorm the freewriting ideas you listed in your journal entry. Brainstorming is listing whatever you know or perhaps feel about your idea. You might add to your freewriting list that you like being outdoors. You would then have the following list related to the kind of work you want to do:

> physical activity
> like sports
> good at sports
> work with people
> work with kids
> work outdoors

Brainstorming can help you identify the major points and supporting details you can use to develop your idea for your essay. From your freewriting and brainstorming lists, for example, you could decide you want to teach sports. Your supporting details could be that you like physical activity, working with people and kids, and being outdoors. Next you need to brainstorm the kind of training you think you need. Your list might look like this:

> physical education
> physical therapy (maybe)
> teaching education
> teacher certification (maybe)

games and game rules
emergency care, CPR

You have now identified the two major points of your essay: the kind of work you want to do and the training you think you need for that work. From your brainstorming lists, you have also defined the supporting details you can use.

Keeping a journal encourages your writing and helps you to focus on and to write about your ideas. A journal is also an important tool for you to use in your work. A record of events, meetings, and your observations related to your work can provide you with helpful reminders and documentation if you need to prepare a report, speech, letter, or memo.

The Essay

An essay is a prose composition about a single subject. An essay consists of an introductory paragraph, several developmental paragraphs (the body of the essay), and a concluding paragraph. Although the main idea (thesis) may be stated anywhere in the essay, generally you should state the main idea or thesis of your essay in the introductory paragraph. The body of the essay consists of the paragraphs in which the major points (the topic of each paragraph) that support the main idea and the supporting details for each major point are developed. In the concluding paragraph, you should restate the thesis and perhaps sum up the major supporting points. The following chart shows the organization of an essay:

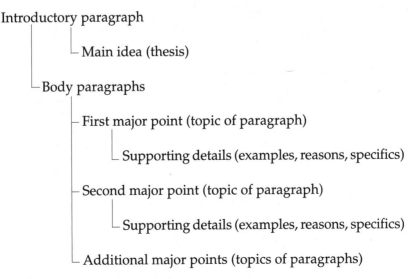

Introductory paragraph
  └ Main idea (thesis)

└ Body paragraphs
    ├ First major point (topic of paragraph)
    │   └ Supporting details (examples, reasons, specifics)
    ├ Second major point (topic of paragraph)
    │   └ Supporting details (examples, reasons, specifics)
    └ Additional major points (topics of paragraphs)

Concluding paragraph

Notice, for example, that the writer of "Living to Work," Dorothy L. Sayers, states her main idea in the first paragraph: people are divided into two main groups when it comes to what they think about work. Although she does not identify the two groups in that paragraph, she defines the two groups in the second paragraph: those who consider work as a "hateful necessity" and those who consider work "enjoyment and self-fulfillment." The topics of the third and fourth paragraphs are the "hateful necessity" and "enjoyment and self-fulfillment" groups, respectively, and examples of the people who make up each group. In the fifth and final paragraph, the writer expands on the main idea and concludes the essay.

Read the following essay, "Living to Work," by Dorothy L. Sayers. Look at the analyses of the organization and content of the essay in the left margin.

Introductory paragraph Main idea (thesis)	When I look at the world—not particularly at the world at war, but at our Western civilization generally—I find myself dividing people into two main groups according to the way they think about work. And I feel sure that the new world after the war will be satisfactory or not according to the view we are all prepared to take about the work of the world. So let us look for a moment at these two groups of people.
Body paragraph Definition of two groups	One group—probably the larger and certainly the more discontented—look upon work as a hateful necessity, whose only use is to make money for them, so that they can escape from work and do something else. They feel that only when the day's labor is over can they really begin to live and be themselves. The other group—smaller nowadays, but on the whole far happier—look on their work as an opportunity for enjoyment and self-fulfillment. They only want to make money so that they may be free to devote themselves more singlemindedly to their work. Their work and their life are one thing; if they were to be cut off from their work, they would feel that they were cut off from life. You will realize that we have here a really fundamental difference of outlook, which is bound to influence all schemes about work, leisure and wages.
Major point (topic of paragraph) Body paragraph	Now the first group—that of the work-haters—is not made up solely of people doing very hard, uninteresting and ill-paid work. It includes a great many well-off people who do practically no work at all. The rich man who lives idly on his income, the man who gambles or speculates in the hope of making money without working for it, the woman who marries for the mere sake of being comfortably established for life—all these people look on money in the same way: as something that saves them from the curse of work. Except that they have had better luck, their outlook is exactly the same as that of the sweated factory hand whose daily work

Supporting details	is one long round of soul-and-body-destroying toil. For all of them, work is something hateful, only to be endured because it makes money; and money is desirable because it represents a way of escape from work. The only difference is that the rich have already made their escape, and the poor have not.
Topic of paragraph	The second group is equally mixed. It includes the artists, scholars and scientists—the people really devoured with the passion for making and discovering things. It includes also—
Body paragraph	and this is very important—those skilled mechanics and engineers who are genuinely in love with the complicated beauty of the machines they use and look after. Then there are those professional people in whom we recognize a clear, spiritual vocation—a call to what is sometimes very hard and exacting work—those doctors, nurses, priests, actors, teachers, whose work is something more to them than a mere means of livelihood; seamen who, for all they may grumble at the hardships of the sea, return to it again and again and are restless and unhappy on dry land; farmers and farm-workers who devotedly serve the land and the beasts they tend; airmen; explorers; and those comparatively rare women to whom the nurture of children is not merely a natural func-
Supporting details	tion but also a full-time and absorbing intellectual and emotional interest. A very mixed bag, you will notice, and not exclusively confined to the "possessing [classes]," or even to those who, individually or collectively, "own the means of production." . . .
Concluding paragraph	We have *all* become accustomed to rate the value of work by a purely money standard. The people who still cling to the idea that work should be served and enjoyed for its own sake are diminishing and—what is worse—are being steadily pushed out of the control of public affairs and out of contact with the public. We find them odd and alien—and a subservient journalism (which we encourage by buying and reading it) persuades us to consider them absurd and con-
Expansion of main idea	temptible. It is only in times of emergency and national disaster that we realize how much we depend upon the man who puts the integrity of his job before money, before success, before self—before all those standards by which we have come to assess the value of work.

The Summary

A summary is a condensed explanation, in your own words, of the essential information in an essay, article, report, speech, story, book, or other communication. Regardless of the form or length of the original communication, a summary is limited to the essential idea in the original communication. In a summary, you should:

- Identify the title and author of the communication being summarized.
- State, in your own words, the following:
  - Main idea (thesis)
  - Major supporting points
  - Significant supporting details

Look at the following summary of "Living to Work" and notice how it follows these requirements:

> In "Living to Work," Dorothy L. Sayers says that our view of work will determine the nature of our world. One group, the "work haters," views their work as only a necessity to earn the money to live. The second group, a smaller group, enjoys their work and finds it fulfilling. According to Sayers, we have become used to rating work by a money standard and to considering those who enjoy their work as odd. However, says Sayers, when we are faced with an emergency or a disaster, we depend on those persons who attach value and integrity to their work.

The ability to write a summary is useful to you in many ways. First, summarizing increases your understanding of the materials you read because to summarize, you must identify the significant ideas and the relationships among those ideas. What is the main idea of the communication? What are the major points the writer used to support the main idea? And what are the significant details that support the major points? Second, a summary of another writer's ideas may be included in support of your opinion in compositions such as essays, reports, or research papers. You must, of course, give credit to the writer whose ideas you include. If you quote the other writer's words, you must enclose them in quotation marks.

As you proceed through the chapters that follow, you will see that the requirements of the journal, essay, and summary are applicable to minutes of meetings, research notes, abstracts, executive summaries, letters, reports, and other business writing forms. You will also see that the ability to analyze an article, report, or other written document is essential to both your academic career and to your later success in your chosen work.

What You Do Is What You Are

Nickie McWhirter

*After graduation from the University of Michigan, Nickie McWhirter
began her career as a feature writer for the* Detroit Free Press *and later
became a columnist for the same paper.*

Before You Read

What do you think of a person who is a doctor? A lawyer? A sales
clerk? A musician? A baseball, basketball, or football player?

Words to Know

anthropologist   a person who studies the characteristics,
   customs, and relationships of humankind

entrepreneur   a person who starts and manages a business
   undertaking

phenomenon   an unusual or strange occurrence

validate   confirm

Americans, unlike people almost everywhere else in the world, tend to   1
define and judge everybody in terms of the work they do, especially work
performed for pay. Charlie is a doctor; Sam is a carpenter; Mary Ellen is a
copywriter at a small ad agency. It is as if by defining how a person earns
his or her rent money, we validate or reject that person's existence. Through
the work and job title, we evaluate the worth of the life attached. Larry is
a laid-off auto worker; Tony is a retired teacher; Sally is a former showgirl
and blackjack dealer from Vegas. It is as if by learning that a person currently earns no money at a job—and maybe hasn't earned any money at a
job for years—we assign that person to limbo, at least for the present. We
define such nonemployed persons in terms of their past job history.

   This seems peculiar to me. People aren't cast in bronze because of the   2
jobs they hold or once held. A retired teacher, for example, may spend a
lot of volunteer time working with handicapped children or raising money
for the Loyal Order of Hibernating Hibiscus. That apparently doesn't
count. Who's Tony? A retired teacher. A laid-off auto worker may pump
gas at his cousin's gas station or sell encyclopedias on weekends. But
who's Larry? Until and unless he begins to work steadily again, he's a
laid-off auto worker. This is the same as saying he's nothing now, but he
used to be something: an auto worker.

There is a whole category of other people who are "just" something.   3
To be "just" anything is the worst. It is not to be recognized by society as
having much value at all, not now and probably not in the past either. To
be "just" anything is to be totally discounted, at least for the present.
There are lots of people who are "just" something. "Just" a housewife
immediately and painfully comes to mind. We still hear it all the time.
Sometimes women who have kept a house and reared six children refer
to themselves as "'just' a housewife." "Just" a bum, "just" a kid, "just" a
drunk, bag lady, old man, student, punk are some others. You can probably add to the list. The "just" category contains present non-earners,
people who have no past job history highly valued by society and people
whose present jobs are on the low-end of pay and prestige scales. A person can be "just" a cab driver, for example, or "just" a janitor. No one is
ever "just" a vice-president, however.

We're supposed to be a classless society, but we are not. We don't rec-   4
ognize a titled nobility. We refuse to acknowledge dynastic privilege. But
we certainly separate the valued from the valueless, and it has a lot to do
with jobs and the importance or prestige we attach to them.

It is no use arguing whether any of this is correct or proper. Rationally   5
it is silly. That's our system, however, and we should not only keep it in
mind, we should teach our children how it works. It is perfectly swell to
want to grow up to be a cowboy or a nurse. Kids should know, however,
that quite apart from earnings potential, the cattle breeder is much more
respected than the hired hand. The doctor gets a lot more respect and
privilege than the nurse.

I think some anthropologist ought to study our uncataloged system of   6
awarding respect and deference to each other based on jobs we hold.
Where does a vice-president–product planning fit in? Is that better than
vice-president–sales in the public consciousness, or unconsciousness?
Writers earn diddly dot, but I suspect they are held in higher esteem than
wealthy rock musicians—that is, if everybody older than 40 gets to vote.

How do we decide which jobs have great value and, therefore, the job-   7
holders are wonderful people? Why is someone who builds shopping
centers called an entrepreneur while someone who builds freeways is
called a contractor? I have no answers to any of this, but we might think
about the phenomenon the next time we are tempted to fawn over some
stranger because we find out he happens to be a judge, or the next time
we catch ourselves discounting the personal worth of the garbage collector.

Questions About the Reading

1. What is the main idea or thesis of the essay? Does the writer state the thesis directly? If so, in which paragraph of the essay is it stated?
2. How do we classify retired people, according to the writer?
3. Does the writer seem to think we hold a person in higher esteem based only on the amount of money the person earns? What does she say that helped you decide your answer?

Thinking Critically

1. What do you think are the criteria by which people decide the esteem or rank in our society of a particular occupation?
2. What are the occupations you classify as high, medium, and low in esteem or rank in our society? What criteria did you use to rank the occupations?
3. Do you think a person's work is significant in determining the person's character? Or do you think a person's character is significant in her or his choice of work?

Writing Assignments

1. In your journal, assess your own personal qualities in terms of responsibility, self-esteem, sociability, integrity, and honesty.
2. Write a summary of the essay.
3. Write an essay explaining which personal qualities—responsibility, self-esteem, sociability, integrity, and honesty—are most important for success as a student, a teacher, and a business manager.

Work and Play

Robert Murray Davis

A father and son may have different ideas about how to define work, as Robert Murray Davis tells us in this essay from his book Mid-Lands: A Family Album *about growing up in a small town in Missouri.*

Before You Read

Do you and your parents have different ideas about what is work and what is play?

Words to Know

diffidence   hesitancy
impertinent   forward, presumptuous

Late in the afternoon on a hot August day in 1957, I had come home   1
after a summer of working on my master's thesis before leaving to study
for a doctorate. The thick walls of the house and the high ceiling of the
living room shut out most of the heat, and I sat in an easy chair, a notepad
on one arm, a bourbon and water over ice on the other, a book in my lap.

My father entered the front door and came through the hall into the   2
living room. He was hot. He may have remembered his father reading
novels instead of tending to any business at all. He was moving, and I
was sitting down. He slowed, but didn't stop, and said, "When you going to get off your ass and do some work?"

Nearly twenty-three, I was used to carrying on a conversation with a   3
moving target. "I *am* working, Dad. This is what I do when I work."

"Bullshit!" And he disappeared through the door to the dining room   4
on his way to the kitchen.

Ten years later, a not-so-young assistant professor trying to publish   5
enough to make a name for myself, I stopped at the door of the
department's senior professor and most distinguished scholar to say hello.
With the kind of diffidence that comes from complete confidence, he said,
"I hope you won't think I'm impertinent, but some of us are concerned
that you are working so hard that you will injure your health."

I thanked him for his concern, assured him that I felt fine, and added,   6
"I can't wait to tell my father that, but I'm not going to tell him over the
phone. I want to see his face." With Dad, you had to be able to read faint
signs. He almost never laughed, and he rarely smiled. But when I told

him the story, his lip twitched just a little. Perhaps he didn't remember what Grandpa Murray said on hearing him praised for being hard-working: "Well, it's no wonder. He got enough rest when he was young."

More than ten years later, several days into my annual visit, Dad and I 7 were looking out over his lawn. I noticed that the large lilac bush by the fence between lawn and pasture was full of volunteer maple trees, and I went over and pulled up some of the smaller ones. Soon I had a trimming saw and tree-trimming tool and had moved out of the lilac bush to take care of the fencerow. Dad finally got his electric saw and took care of the thickest trunks. After a while, we were dusty, scratched a little here and there, and wet through with sweat. But the lilac bush and fence were a lot cleaner. Still, the pasture side of the fence was littered with debris from our work, and I suggested that we get the tractor and trailer, load up the trash, and take it down to the hollow to retard erosion.

"No," Dad said, "let's leave it for a while." A pause. Then, almost plain- 8 tively, "You worked me too hard."

I raised my eyes to heaven and said, only part mockingly, "Thank you, 9 God!" I had become an adult.

Dad wasn't always as grim as he might sound or as serious as he may 10 have felt he had to be to set the right example. In fact, I began to suspect that he regarded life not just as a test but a series of contests. He had done a lot of things, and it was always a dilemma what to put down in the blanks after "father's occupation." "Trader" seemed to connote the South Seas. "Dealer" was OK until the current connotation got locked in. What he actually did, or did best, was buy and sell things: cars, cattle, farm machinery, almost anything that wasn't nailed down and some things that were. When I was a boy it seemed that Dad made play seem like work. And work was deadly serious. When I got old enough to tease him—about age thirty-five—I told him that his motto ought to be, "If it feels good, you must be doing it wrong." When concentrating on a physi-cal or mechanical job, he would stick his tongue between his teeth at one edge of his mouth and frown in concentration. My major contribution to repair jobs was holding the flashlight while mysterious stuff went on in the bowels of whatever it was. Every job was a test with no make-up. The worst beating I ever got—bad enough that it was the last—was because, even though I had not been told to, I had fed the pigs on my own initia-tive. (At least that was the only reason I was ever given. Having since been a parent myself, I wonder if something else might not have been going on.)

Looking back, I can see that Dad was more intense than anything else. 11 It was always surprising to find that he could play. For Christmas (of 1941, I think) he got me a full electric train set, the better for being used because the tracks were already mounted on big boards, which he set up in the basement of the duplex on Fourth Street and played with for hours to wind down after a run on the Katy. Later he would sometimes stop by the basketball goal he had installed under the walnut trees, call for the ball, and throw it up, while moving, the kind of two-handed underhand shot popular in his high school days. I remember his playing catch with me only once, when he demonstrated how to throw a curveball. For several days afterward he moved his right arm carefully, and as with various other situations, I sympathize more now than I did then. But the only time he really surprised me was at his wholesale fruit and vegetable business. We were unloading a truckload of watermelons, and Dad promised that if one got broken, we could take it home. We had almost finished, with no damage, and I was starting to worry. Dad looked over the few remaining, hefted the most promising knee-high, looked at me, grinned slightly, lowered the melon to shin level, and dropped it. It may not have been the best-tasting melon I ever had, but it was the most satisfying.

My father taught me almost everything about work—finally, even, that it could be more fun than nominal play—except how to do what he did, and that was because, knowing I was incompetent, I didn't even try to learn. In fact, the fathers of my contemporaries did not pass on this kind of knowledge. Of the boys I can trace from my crowd, only one, a farmer, does anything like what his father did. Or where he did it. The fathers weren't holding out on us; they wanted us to live different lives and finally, I think, my father was pleased that I did. If he never understood what I do when I work, he was glad to have a son clever enough to get away with doing whatever it was and energetic enough to do a lot of it. If it was a bluff, it was a bluff a good card player could respect.

Because he went to bed about 9:00 P.M., I never managed to get up in the morning before he did. But I get up a lot earlier and more voluntarily than I used to, I go to work a lot more willingly, and I enjoy doing it a lot more than I do most forms of play. He didn't necessarily want me to go out and clear that last fencerow, but I suspect that despite his exhaustion he was pleased that I hadn't forgotten how to do a job that wasn't mine without having to be told and how to insist on carrying it through to the end.

Later I told the story to his oldest surviving friend and added, "Working for Dad makes every job I've had since look easy." Dad snorted, and I don't know whether or not he believed me. He should have. And it should have pleased him.

———————————

Questions About the Reading

1. What is the father's opinion of his son's choice of work? What is the writer's opinion of his father's work?
2. What is the main idea of the essay? State it in your own words.
3. What did his father do when they were at his fruit and vegetable business that surprised the writer?

Thinking Critically

1. Is planting flowers, as an example, harder work than writing, or is writing harder work than planting flowers?
2. What occupations do you think are hard work? Why?
3. In choosing your future work, are the physical or intellectual requirements more important to you?

Writing Assignments

1. Write a summary of the essay.
2. Choose an occupation that you think has significant physical requirements and explain, in an essay, why you would or would not like to work in that occupation.
3. Choose an occupation, such as an engineer, that you think of as requiring extensive education and training in determining the resources (time, materials, money, space, staff) needed to produce a product (a car, for example). Explain in an essay why you would or would not like that occupation.

My Mother Never Worked

Bonnie Smith-Yackel

Bonnie Smith-Yackel's family survived on a farm during the Great Depression, a time when both the weather and the economy made the hardships of farm life nearly overwhelming. In this personal essay, Smith-Yackel uses the example of her mother's life to reveal the unfairness in American society's attitudes toward women and the work they do to keep their families going.

Before You Read

Why do you think the government does not grant homemakers the same rights as workers employed outside the home?

Words to Know

cholera   a contagious, often fatal disease, usually restricted to farm animals in the United States

reciprocated   returned

sustenance   nourishment, support for life

widow's pension   the Social Security payments given to a widow, based on her deceased husband's eligibility, who is not eligible herself for Social Security

———————

"**S**ocial Security Office." (The voice answering the telephone sounds 1 very self-assured.)

"I'm calling about . . . I . . . my mother just died . . . I was told to call you 2 and see about a . . . death-benefit check, I think they call it. . . ."

"I see. Was your mother on Social Security? How old was she?"   3

"Yes . . . she was seventy-eight. . . ."   4

"Do you know her number?"   5

"No . . . I, ah . . . don't you have a record?"   6

"Certainly. I'll look it up. Her name?"   7

"Smith. Martha Smith. Or maybe she used Martha Ruth Smith. . . .   8 Sometimes she used her maiden name . . . Martha Jerabek Smith."

"If you'd care to hold on, I'll check our records—it'll be a few min-   9 utes."

"Yes. . . ."   10

Her love letters—to and from Daddy—were in an old box, tied with 11 ribbons and stiff, rigid-with-age leather thongs: 1918 through 1920; hers written on stationery from the general store she had worked in full-time and managed, single-handed, after her graduation from high school in 1913; and his, at first, on YMCA or Soldiers and Sailors Club stationery dispensed to the fighting men of World War I. He wooed her thoroughly and persistently by mail, and though she reciprocated all his feelings for her, she dreaded marriage. . . .

"It's so hard for me to decide when to have my wedding day—that's 12 all I've thought about these last two days. I have told you dozens of times that I won't be afraid of married life, but when it comes down to setting the date and then picturing myself a married woman with half a dozen or more kids to look after, it just makes me sick. . . . I am weeping right now—I hope that some day I can look back and say how foolish I was to dread it all."

They married in February, 1921, and began farming. Their first baby, a 13 daughter, was born in January, 1922, when my mother was 26 years old. The second baby, a son, was born in March, 1923. They were renting farms; my father, besides working his own fields, also was a hired man for two other farmers. They had no capital initially, and had to gain it slowly, working from dawn until midnight every day. My town-bred mother learned to set hens and raise chickens, feed pigs, milk cows, plant and harvest a garden, and can every fruit and vegetable she could scrounge. She carried water nearly a quarter of a mile from the well to fill her wash boilers in order to do her laundry on a scrub board. She learned to shuck grain, feed threshers, shuck and husk corn, feed corn pickers. In September, 1925, the third baby came, and in June, 1927, the fourth child—both daughters. In 1930, my parents had enough money to buy their own farm, and that March they moved all their livestock and belongings themselves, 55 miles over rutted, muddy roads.

In the summer of 1930 my mother and her two eldest children reclaimed 14 a 40-acre field from Canadian thistles, by chopping them all out with a hoe. In the other fields, when the oats and flax began to head out, the green and blue of the crops were hidden by the bright yellow of wild mustard. My mother walked the fields day after day, pulling each mustard plant. She raised a new flock of baby chicks—500—and she spaded up, planted, hoed, and harvested a half-acre garden.

During the next spring their hogs caught cholera and died. No cash 15 that fall.

And in the next year the drought hit. My mother and father trudged 16 from the well to the chickens, the well to the calf pasture, the well to the barn, and from the well to the garden. The sun came out hot and bright, endlessly, day after day. The crops shriveled and died. They harvested half the corn, and ground the other half, stalks and all, and fed it to the cattle as fodder. With the price at four cents a bushel for the harvested crop, they couldn't afford to haul it into town. They burned it in the furnace for fuel that winter.

In 1934, in February, when the dust was still so thick in the Minnesota 17 air that my parents couldn't always see from the house to the barn, their fifth child—a fourth daughter—was born. My father hunted rabbits daily, and my mother stewed them, fried them, canned them, and wished out loud that she could taste hamburger once more. In the fall the shotgun brought prairie chickens, ducks, pheasant, and grouse. My mother plucked each bird, carefully reserving the breast feathers for pillows.

In the winter she sewed night after night, endlessly, begging cast-off 18 clothing from relatives, ripping apart coats, dresses, blouses, and trousers to remake them to fit her four daughters and son. Every morning and every evening she milked cows, fed pigs and calves, cared for chickens, picked eggs, cooked meals, washed dishes, scrubbed floors, and tended and loved her children. In the spring she planted a garden once more, dragging pails of water to nourish and sustain the vegetables for the family. In 1936 she lost a baby in her sixth month.

In 1937 her fifth daughter was born. She was 42 years old. In 1939 a 19 second son, and in 1941 her eighth child—and third son.

But the war had come, and prosperity of a sort. The herd of cattle had 20 grown to 30 head; she still milked morning and evening. Her garden was more than a half acre—the rains had come, and by now the Rural Electricity Administration and indoor plumbing. Still she sewed—dresses and jackets for the children, house dresses and aprons for herself, weekly patching of jeans, overalls, and denim shirts. Still she made pillows, using the feathers she had plucked, and quilts every year—intricate patterns as well as patchwork, stitched as well as tied—all necessary bedding for her family. Every scrap of cloth too small to be used in quilts was carefully saved and painstakingly sewed together in strips to make rugs. She still went out in the fields to help with the haying whenever there was a threat of rain.

In 1959 my mother's last child graduated from high school. A year 21 later the cows were sold. She still raised chickens and ducks, plucked feathers, made pillows, baked her own bread, and every year made a new quilt—now for a married child or for a grandchild. And her garden, that huge, undying symbol of sustenance, was as large and cared for as in all the years before. The canning, and now freezing, continued.

In 1969, on a June afternoon, mother and father started out for town so 22 that she could buy sugar to make rhubarb jam for a daughter who lived in Texas. The car crashed into a ditch. She was paralyzed from the waist down.

In 1970 her husband, my father, died. My mother struggled to regain 23
some competence and dignity and order in her life. At the rehabilitation
institute, where they gave her physical therapy and trained her to live
usefully in a wheelchair, the therapist told me: "She did fifteen pushups
today—fifteen! She's almost seventy-five years old! I've never known a
woman so strong!"

Form her wheelchair she canned pickles, baked bread, ironed clothes, 24
wrote dozens of letters weekly to her friends and her "half dozen or more
kids," and made three patchwork housecoats and one quilt. She made
balls and balls of carpet rags—enough for five rugs. And kept all her love
letters.

"I think I've found your mother's records—Martha Ruth Smith; mar- 25
ried to Ben F. Smith?"

"Yes, that's right."   26
"Well, I see that she was getting a widow's pension. . . ."   27
"Yes, that's right."   28
"Well, your mother isn't entitled to our $255 death benefit."   29
"Not entitled! But why?"   30
The voice on the telephone explains patiently: 31
"Well, you see—your mother never worked."   32

Questions About the Reading

1. Why didn't the writer's mother want to get married?
2. In her later years, how do you think Mrs. Smith's attitude had changed
   from the one she expressed in the letter quoted in paragraph 12. What
   had become of her fears of marriage?
3. Why did Mrs. Smith do the pushups, and why did she continue to
   work in her final years, when she really didn't have to?
4. Do you believe women like Mrs. Smith deserve Social Security? Explain your answer.

Thinking Critically

1. How would you compare the demands of housework and raising children to working on an automobile assembly line? Do they require the
   same or different personal qualities?
2. Which of the five competencies identified inside the cover of this book
   are needed to manage a household?

Writing Assignments

1. Write an essay in which you give examples of the decisions that have to be made in managing a home.
2. Write an essay in which you give examples of the obstacles that have to be overcome in the working world.

Working Just to Live Is Perverted into Living Just to Work

Ana Veciana-Suarez

Ana Veciana-Suarez is a family columnist for the Miami Herald. *In this essay, she asks us to consider whether work should be allowed to take over one's family and personal life.*

Before You Read

How do you plan to balance the requirements of your work and your personal life?

Words to Know

boundaries   limits

compulsive   driven, compelled

phenomenon   unusual or extraordinary event or occurrence

reconciled   settled, made consistent

simultaneously   at the same time

transformations   changes, alternations

He's hardly ever home. The children are asleep when he leaves for the 1 office, asleep when he returns. He misses most of their activities. On Sundays, if there's no paperwork to finish, no meetings, no community demands, he's too tired to be much fun.

His son learned to fish without him. His daughter became a young 2 woman before he realized it. He turned gray, it seemed, overnight. He gave up tennis and soccer and took up spreadsheets. They sold their pop-up camper because it gathered dirt and leaves in the driveway.

I was told this by someone who knows: his wife. 3

"He has no life," she says matter-of-factly. 4

I imagine she meant something more, too: We have no life together, as 5 a family.

I hear and witness these transformations more than I care to, enough 6 that it has become a regular refrain of mine: We work so hard, so long, that there is often nothing left for us and our families by the end of the day, and certainly not by the end of the week.

We think of this as a new phenomenon, a product of downsizing and 7
corporate mergers. Hardly. A friend sent me the words to "My Little One,"
an 1890s Yiddish song that resounds with concerns of today:

> I have a son, a little son,
> A boy completely fine.
> When I see him it seems to me
> That all the world is mine.
> But seldom, seldom do I see
> My child awake and bright;
> I only see him when he sleeps;
> I'm only home at night.
> It's early when I leave for work;
> When I return it's late.
> Unknown to me is my own flesh,
> Unknown is my child's face . . .

A century later, we are stuck in an endless, destructive cycle, simulta- 8
neously addicted to and repulsed by our work, at once proud of our long
hours and frightened by what they mean. Even as we are compulsive in
chasing the next career rung, many of us profess to be burned out.

Are we confused, or delusional?   9

I'm not sure. I used to believe that my generation was disillusioned 10
with the demands and the emotional price tag of their fathers' careers
and would change things. But as we approach middle age, when the psychological commitments of child-rearing and family care-taking inten-
sify, work for many has become an end in itself and a means to get away
from our homes and ourselves.

Sure, some work long and hard of necessity. Most of those I know, 11
though, work more to make more money to buy more and bigger things.
We want, we want, we want. So we work, we work, we work.

The job comes to do more than define us. It owns us. We live to work, 12
and as a result, the job comes with us whoever we are—by fax at home,
by beeper at the ballet recital, by cellular phone in the car. We have become so efficient—we expect ourselves to be so efficient—that work is no
longer something we do solely in an office. Those boundaries have been
erased.

So we answer client mail between innings at our son's games. We jot 13
notes for tomorrow's job presentation while our toddler plays in her sand-
box. We organize our briefcase in the pediatrician's waiting room.

I love my job. I love putting together the words, the turn of phrase, 14
that will make a reader savor the sound of language. I wonder, though,
after drifting back from columnland into my children's conversations, if
I'm turning over too much of me. Or maybe the question really is: Am I
giving up too much of them for my own pleasure and ambition?

Part of the problem stems, I believe, from the way we describe the 15 integration of our work and family lives, with words that imply we can do both well if only we organize, prioritize, set our minds to it. Juggle this. Balance that.

Conspicuously absent in discussions is the admission that much of life 16 turns out to be a series of either-or choices, not merely a matter of better management or improved organization.

We don't talk so readily of giving up, putting aside—and maybe that's 17 exactly what we need to do.

Some competing demands can't be reconciled. Sometimes, we need to 18 surrender some of our ambition. That's life, or at the least the life we all claim we want to live. Because if we're not careful, our sons will learn to fish alone and our daughters will grow up before we know it.

Questions About the Reading

1. What is the main idea of the essay? Is it stated? If so, where?
2. According to the writer, why do most people work more?
3. According to the writer, how long have people been working so hard and so long? What is the example she uses to support her statement that it is not a new phenomenon?
4. What does the writer suggest as a solution to the "living just to work" problem?

Thinking Critically

1. If your choice of a career required long working hours, how would you balance those hours and your family and personal life?
2. What would you do if you had to choose between staying after work for an important meeting and going to a family reunion or wedding?
3. If your choice of a career required frequent travel out of town, how would you manage your family and personal life?

Writing Assignments

1. In your journal, identify the factors that are important to you in choosing your future work.
2. Write an essay in which you explain the goals you have related to your future work. Evaluate any conflicting risks or demands your goals might impose on your family, friends, and personal life. Suggest how you would balance the conflicts.

2

Choosing a Career

Do you think you know what career you want, or are you, like most students, not yet sure? In "Choices: Vocation, Career, or Job," Alan M. Webber asks the directors of the masters in business administration programs at Harvard Business School for advice on making career choices.

Depending on your career choice, you may need to follow a liberal arts, vocational, technical, or cooperative education path. The values of each path have long been debated by students and scholars. Rebecca Knight, in "Liberal Arts Gave Me a Liberal Dose of Life Lessons," is a strong supporter of her liberal arts education. In "Different Paths to Success," Joannie M. Schrof tells us about three students who chose the vocational/technical education path to successful employment. In "Cooperative Education: Learn More, Earn More, Prepare for the Workplace," Matthew Mariani points to the value of a cooperative education path.

But how do you know what kind of work you should choose? Barbara Moses, in "Find Work That You Love," provides some guidelines and suggests twelve rules to follow for success in the career you choose.

In this chapter you will be asked to interpret a table of information and to develop a table. You will also be asked to write several different kinds of reports. Some of the reports will be written in collaboration with classmates. Collaboration—working with others—is essential in the working world. The successful Mars Pathfinder mission, for example, was the result of the collaboration of diverse specialists. Today, the design and production of a new car model is the result of a collaborative group of engineers and other specialists.

Collaboration involves the interpersonal skills of listening, communicating, working with people of diverse backgrounds, contributing to the

group, leading, and negotiating. Once the members of the group are determined, you will want to meet to define, organize, and schedule the
project. One member may emerge as the leader, or the group may choose
a leader to coordinate the project. Each member should be responsible
for some part of the project and for meeting the schedule that is set.

The Table

A table consists of information displayed in columns and rows. Columns
list information vertically; rows list information horizontally. Each column and each row should be labeled as to the information it contains.
The information may be numbers or words. The table should be titled
and, if more than one table is included in a document, the tables should
be numbered consecutively (1, 2, 3, and so on).

In this chapter, you will be asked to develop tables, similar to the following table, which is from America's Career INFONET Web site. The
table gives employment trends for medical assistants in the United States
and California. Notice that each column and each row is titled. The column on the left is called the *stub* and identifies the information that follows across each row.

Occupation Report

Occupation: Medical assistants
State: California
Typical Educational Level: Moderate-term on-the-job training
Description: Perform various duties under the direction of physician in
examination and treatment of patients. Prepare treatment room, maintain inventory of supplies and instruments, and set up patient for attention of physician. Hand instruments and materials to physician as
directed. Schedule appointments, keep medical records, and perform sec-
retarial duties.

Trends:

Location	Employment		Per-centage change	Average annual job openings (due to growth and net replacement)
	1996	2006		
United States	224,800	391,200	74%	21,000
California	36,000	60,600	68%	3,400

Source: Bureau of Labor Statistics, 1996; California Employment Development Department, Labor Market Information

You can develop tables on your computer by using the "Table" command. The command permits you to specify the number of columns and rows you want and displays an empty table in which you can fill in the information you want.

The Report

A report is an informative, factual, objective account based on research, investigation, or observation. Reports are used to provide accident, progress, travel, policy, sales figures, or other information of significance to the managers or employees of a business or to the members of an organization.

There are many kinds of reports: long, short, formal, informal. A short, informal report may be written as a memo, letter, or e-mail, as you will see in Chapters 4, 5, and 7 and several writing assignments. Within an organization—a police department, for example—special reporting forms may be provided. A long, formal report will generally require a table of contents and an abstract or executive summary as part of the report. A report may or may not include the writer's opinion or recommendations.

A short, informal report should include the following:

- Date
- Subject
- Headings

The headings should identify the subdivisions of the report. Tables or other visual aids (bullets—as above—or numbering) are often included in a report to set off and clarify information. The following is an example of a park employee's report in response to an assignment by a supervisor to investigate the number of persons using the exercise paths in the local park. Notice that the report is headed by the date and its subject and that it contains headings identifying the parts or divisions of the report. A table provides the requested information.

The headings within a report depend on the nature and content of the specific report, but the subject and opening paragraph of the report should state clearly what the report is about—much as you would state the thesis of an essay in its opening paragraph.

A formal report, usually several pages in length, is generally based on a research project or investigation and requires, in addition to the report itself, a title page, table of contents, and abstract. Extensive reports prepared for an executive in a company or organization will generally include an executive summary. An executive summary is generally several paragraphs in length because of the extent of the report.

Date: March 30, 2000

Subject: Number and Kind of Exercisers in North Street Park, 8:00–
                 9:00 A.M.

Purpose: The purpose of my investigation was to determine the
                 number of persons exercising in North Street Park between
                 8:00 and 9:00 A.M. and thus determine the need for more
                 exercise paths.

Number and Kind of Exercisers:

	Walkers	Bikers	Runners	Rollerbladers	Others
8:00–8:30	50	25	30	20	9
8:30–9:00	63	32	26	16	14
	113	57	56	36	23

Observations: From 8:00–8:30, 134 exercisers were using the paths. From
                 8:30–9:00, there were 151. The "other" exercisers were par-
                 ents running behind strollers containing children. At all
                 times, the number of bikers, runners, rollerbladers, and
                 "others" created a dangerous situation for the walkers and
                 themselves because of the limited number and width of
                 the paths.

Recommendation:
                 My recommendation is that the number and width of the
                 paths be increased. Consideration should be given to cre-
                 ating a path for the walkers and the "others," and a dif-
                 ferent path for the bikers, runners, and rollerbladers.

The title page includes the title of the report, date of the report, and
name of the author of the report. Generally, this information is listed in
capital letters, with the title printed in the middle and center of the page
and the date and author toward the bottom of the page. The table of contents lists each heading and subheading included in the report, with their
beginning page numbers, as well as any tables or illustrations included
in the report.

Although technical differences can exist between a summary and an
abstract, to prepare an abstract, you need to use the summarizing skills

you learned in Chapter 1. The important point to remember is that the purpose of the abstract is to provide your reader with a condensed account, like a summary, of the report's significant information. An abstract will generally be a single paragraph.

The following is an abbreviated example of a formal report.

NORTH STREET PARK RENOVATION PROJECT

A FEASIBILITY STUDY

APRIL 20, 2000

GEORGE A. PARKINTON

Contents

List of Tables

ABSTRACT

During 1999, injuries were sustained by eighteen persons exercising on the paths in North Street Park. Following observations
of the use of the exercise paths in North Street Park over a
period of six months and during each season, the Park Department initiated a feasibility study to determine whether the
number of paths could be increased or widened. This report
determines that additional paths could and should be constructed to separate use by walkers and parents with children
from use by bikers, runners, and rollerbladers.

North Street Park Renovation Project

A Feasibility Study

Background

North Street Park was established in 1965 in response to resi-

dent environmental concerns and desire for a place within the

city where residents could exercise. Several paths were then

constructed through the park for exercise purposes. During

1999, eighteen persons sustained injuries on the paths, which

are narrow and, at points, lack good two-way visibility. The

number of injuries caused residents to request improvements in

the exercise paths and to propose an increase in park-use fees

or that a city bond be floated to pay for the improvements.

To determine the need for renovation of the paths, observations

of the number and kind of exercisers were conducted. Given the

kind of exercising and the number of exercisers using the paths

at different hours and during different seasons, this feasibility

study was conducted to determine whether the number of paths

should be increased, whether the existing paths should be wid-

ened, or whether both additional paths and widening of the

existing paths should be undertaken.

1

Problem

Description of Existing Paths

A main path that was constructed originally to accommodate
two persons walking abreast winds through the park. At points,
shrubbery prevents a clear view of persons who may be ap-
proaching. The paths branching off from the main path lead
only to the swimming pool, children's playground, and
parking lot.

Volume of Use

Since the establishment of the park and construction of the
paths, the volume of use of the paths has increased dramatically. The paths are now used not only by walkers but also by
bikers, runners, rollerbladers, and even by parents running
behind strollers containing their children, identified as "others."
During only one morning hour, the following use was
observed:

Table 1: Number of Exercisers

	Walkers	Bikers	Runners	Rollerbladers	Others
8:00–8:30	50	25	30	20	9
8:30–9:00	63	32	26	16	14
	113	57	56	36	23

2

Although use is less heavy during the middle of the day, the

above numbers are typical of each morning until approximately

11:00 A.M. and each evening from about 4:00 to 9:00 P.M.

Injuries in 1999

Of the eighteen injuries sustained in 1999, ten were serious and

required treatment or hospitalization. In each case, a bicycler or

a rollerblader ran into a walker or a parent running with a

stroller. In four of the cases, the accident occurred at one of the

points where visibility was obscured by shrubbery.

Purpose

The purpose of this report is to discuss the results of the study

conducted to determine whether it is feasible to increase the

number of exercise paths through the park, to widen the exist-

ing paths, and/or to provide different paths for different kinds

of exercise.

Discussion

Description of Path Renovations

1. The existing paths should be widened to accommodate

four persons walking abreast. They should be straight-
ened and shrubbery removed or trimmed at those points
where visibility is limited. These points include those
where paths branch off to the swimming pool and
children's playground. The existing paths should be limited to use by walkers and parents with children.

2. An additional path approximately six feet wide should be
   constructed to accommodate bikers, runners, and
   rollerbladers. This path should be constructed near the
   outside perimeter of the park, which would avoid the
   removal of a large number of trees.

Estimated Cost of the Renovations

1. The cost of widening the existing paths requires some
   tree removal and shrubbery trimming, and the addition
   of approximately 3 feet of blacktop to the existing paths.
   The cost is estimated at $66,000.00. This figure includes
   the following costs:

Table 2: Cost Estimate, Existing Path Widening

Tree Removal	Shrubbery Trimming	Blacktop
$6,000.00	$3,000.00	$57,000.00

4

2. The cost of the additional path for bikers, runners, and rollerbladers is estimated at $100,000.00. This figure includes the following costs:

Table 3: Cost Estimate, New Path

Tree Removal	Shrubbery Removal	Blacktop
$2,000.00	$1,500.00	$96,500.00

Conclusion

The widening of the existing paths and the addition of a path for the use of bikers, runners, and rollerbladers should prevent future injuries. The project will also respond to resident requests for additional and improved exercise facilities in the North Street Park. Residents have expressed a willingness to pay increased fees or to support a city-issued bond for this purpose.

Choices: Vocation, Career, or Job

Alan M. Webber

In this interview, business psychologists Timothy Butler and James Waldroop, directors of the masters in business administration programs at the Harvard Business School and co-founders of Waldroop Butler Associates, offer advice on making career choices that will provide both success and satisfaction. An extended version of the interview may be found at www.fastcompany.com/youdecide.

Before You Read

What factors have you considered in choosing the kind of work that you want to do?

Words to Know

dynamic   powerful, forceful

geothermal   heat of the earth's interior

perceptual   conscious, aware

profound   deep, intensely felt

quantitative analysis   measurement of amounts or percentages
   of components of a substance

It's frequently said that careers are over. Instead, you should expect to 1
hold a series of jobs and to participate in a succession of projects. How
do you see the evolution of the career?

Timothy Butler: There are three words that tend to be used interchange- 2
ably—and shouldn't be. They are "vocation," "career," and "job." Vocation is the most profound of the three, and it has to do with your calling.
It's what you're doing in life that makes a difference for you, that builds
meaning for you, that you can look back on in your later years to see the
impact you've made on the world. A calling is something you have to
listen for. You've got to attune yourself to the message.

Career is the term you hear most often today. A career is a line of work. 3
You can say that your career is to be a lawyer or a securities analyst—but
usually it's not the same as your calling. You can have different careers at
different points in your life.

A job is the most specific and immediate of the three terms. It has to do 4
with who's employing you at the moment and what your job description

is for the next 6 months or so. Trying to describe what your job will be beyond 12 to 18 months from now is very dicey.

James Waldroop: If you look at the derivations of the words "career" 5 and "vocation," you immediately get a feel for the difference between them. Vocation comes from the Latin "vocare," which means "to call." It suggests that you are listening for something that calls out to you, something that is particular to you. "Career" comes originally from the Latin word for cart and later from the Middle French word for racetrack. In other words, you go around and around really fast for a long time—but you never get anywhere.

What advice do you have for people facing a tough choice, one that 6 **could permanently change the direction of their work life?**

Butler: A lot of very bright businesspeople try to solve these decisions 7 in their heads. They want to do the math, come up with the right MBA answer. Am I going to spend a lot of time with my kids? Or am I going to start up this company and commit the 90 hours per week that it will require? What's it going to be?

But there's a better way: Take the decision out of the abstract and the 8 absolute, and instead deal with the immediate and the real. Look at the next two months or four months. What's on the agenda? If you have to be on the road, can your family take the hit for the next few months? And then, in the months after that, can your family get more of your attention? The more you can bring your decisions into the here and now, the more you can stay on top of these dynamic tensions—and even be energized by them.

The biggest decision that people face in the world of work is which 9 **career to choose. What advice do you have for people who aren't sure what their career—or their vocation—should be?**

Waldroop: Good career decisions have to be based not just on your 10 aptitudes but also on your "deep" interests. The most common mistake that people make in their career decisions is to do something because they're "good at it." It's a story I hear all the time. Someone will say to me, "I'm an engineer, but I don't like it." Why did you become an engineer? "I was good at science and math, so people told me I should be an engineer." Did you ever *like* engineering? "No, but it was easy."

The real question is, Where are your deep interests? Think of your in- 11 terests as a deep geothermal pool. Once you tap your interests, you can express them in any number of ways. You may have a particular aptitude—science and math, for instance—but without a deep interest in expressing that aptitude, you'll fail.

Butler: Once you recognize that those deep interests are the best pre- 12
dictor of job satisfaction, the next step is to get in touch with your interest
patterns and connect them with the activities that go on in business. Human interests are quite difficult to measure until we reach our early twenties. At that point, they gel—we can measure and describe them. We each
develop a unique signature of life interests. And that signature remains
virtually constant over time.

There are eight core business functions—not functions like marketing, 13
sales, and finance, but basic activities such as quantitative analysis, perceptual thinking, enterprise control, and creative production. If you look
at your deep interests and think about how your interests can be expressed
in specific business behaviors, then you'll have the elements of a good
career decision.

There's one thing that everyone should do in the course of making a 14
career decision: some reflection. You're going to need some systematic
way of thinking through what you know about yourself, thinking through
those times in your life when you were deeply excited about what you
were doing.

You may come up with a list of times in your life when you were doing 15
apparently different things—but at each of those times, you were deeply
engaged. When you analyze those times, you'll find themes that connect
them. Those themes are your core interests. Thinking about them in a
systematic way gives you the information you need to make a good decision.

Questions About the Reading

1. What are the differences among a vocation, career, and job?
2. What is the advice Butler gives if a person is making a choice that can
   permanently change his or her work life?
3. What is the most common mistake people make in their career decisions? What is the question people must ask themselves when choosing a career?
4. What is the procedure Butler says that everyone should follow in making a career decision?

Thinking Critically

1. What kind of work would you classify as a vocation? As a career? As a
   job?

2. In addition to the factors discussed in the interview, what other factors should you consider in choosing a vocation, a career, and a job?
3. What do you think you are good at? What do you consider your deep interests? Are the activities you are good at the same or different than your deep interests?

Writing Assignments

1. Write a summary of "Choices: Vocation, Career, or Job."
2. Choose an occupation that you would like to know more about. Use the library, Internet, your school career guidance office, or other sources—such as observing or interviewing a person employed in that occupation—to find out what education and training the occupation involves. Write an informal report about the results of your research.

Liberal Arts Gave Me a Liberal Dose of Life Lessons

Rebecca Knight

Rebecca Knight, a recent graduate of Wesleyan University in Middletown, Connecticut, was searching for a job when she wrote this article for USA Today.

Before You Read

What do you think are the main advantages of a liberal arts education?

Words to Know

eclectic   mixed, varied
enigmas   puzzles, riddles
innovative   new, creative
spectrum   range

I'm about to be a college graduate and I've been looking through the   1
want ads. It's not much fun.

Page after page reminds me I don't know how to engineer a bridge,   2
design a cattle-feeding program, plan a city's traffic system, or market a
diet soda.

Perhaps I should regret my choice, four years ago, to attend a liberal-   3
arts college instead of someplace more practical. But I don't.

Some would say that all I have now is a new degree and a twinkle in   4
my eye, that I've a "Seinfeld education" which taught a lot about nothing. In some job interviews, prospective employers eye my résumé sus-
piciously. "Wesleyan," they mutter. "Good school, but what did they teach
you?"

Not a trade, I suppose, nor even a particular set of skills. But what I   5
bring to the job market is just as valuable. These four years have prepared me to survive and prosper and contribute in a world that is going
to change dramatically in the half century ahead. These assets I take with
me:

I take myself seriously. Small colleges pride themselves on nurturing   6
close professor/student relationships—with good reason. One-on-one
interaction with professors sharpened my thinking, taught me to endure

criticism, and encouraged me to take intellectual risks. I take myself seriously because professors took me seriously. In the workplace, I will have confidence in my ideas because they often were tested by fire.

I know how to make the connection. I have studied music, govern- 7 ment, psychology, religion, philosophy, economics, biology, and English. My education taught me to connect ideas and concepts across a broad spectrum, to place theories in context, to find one truth in the light of another. I see traces of Plato's *Republic* in Madison's vision for America in *The Federalist Papers.* I think Freud would find Marx a bore. The breadth of knowledge I now possess seems the right foundation for the depth I'll acquire later.

I see the world as a big place. I come from a small high school in 8 Maine and used to think the world looked like my schoolmates. At Wesleyan, I came to know and admire many people from all over the world. I sang with the Ebony Singers, led by local minister Marichal Monts, who gathered an eclectic group of students to celebrate the gospel tradition. I spent a semester in Kenya, learned Swahili, harvested bananas, and slept on straw in a goat hut.

America's racial composition is changing rapidly. In a few decades, 9 less than half the U.S. population will be Caucasian. My peers and I will face this reality in the working world. The liberal arts college I attended has made me eager for that.

The world can be very small, too. If we grow from our interaction 10 with others, we also learn from time alone. I have discovered the joys and terrors of solitude. Much of my education was just me alone—very alone— wrestling with enigmas from which hard thought was the only escape route. My best teachers challenged me with vexing questions, then trusted me to answer them in the harsh, unforgiving way in which we come to grips with the limits of our own understanding.

I'm realistic. I was taught to look at practical problems in unconven- 11 tional ways and I was encouraged to come up with innovative approaches to solving them. In economics class, I created a currency out of coconuts; I argued cases in "court." Much of learning is driven by creativity and imagination; the working world seems less frightening to me now that I've been liberated from the feasible and probable.

I have not learned everything I'll ever need to know at my liberal arts 12 college, but it's been a great start. And if I ever feel the need to learn how to build a bridge, I have confidence that I can do that, too.

———————

Questions About the Reading

1. What does Knight think she gained from the one-on-one interaction she had with professors at her college?
2. What is the competency she learned from the different subjects she studied?
3. How did her education influence her view of the world?
4. What seems to be the main asset or competency Knight gained from her education?

Thinking Critically

1. Would a liberal arts education satisfy your deep interests?
2. Would a liberal arts education provide training in what you are good at?
3. Which of the skills and competencies required in your chosen career would be provided by a liberal arts education?

Writing Assignments

1. Choose three careers and write an informal report identifying the liberal arts courses required in each.
2. Working with some classmates, write an informal report in which you identify the liberal arts courses required in each career in which each of you is interested.

Different Paths to Success

Joannie M. Schrof

In her article for U.S. News & World report, *Joannie M. Schrof provides several examples of students who chose a vocational/technical education path, and she explains why each student chose that path.*

Before You Read

What are the advantages of a vocational/technical education path?

Words to Know

cachet   mark or stamp of quality or authenticity
culinary   cooking
demean   debase, think inferior
omnibus   collection

Although Cheri Wallis had spent much of her childhood in Belton, Texas,   1
happily tinkering with Model T's and other ancient jalopies, she felt obligated to pursue a college degree rather than simply become a grease monkey. So, when it came time to consider colleges in 1989, Wallis planned to enroll at one of the many campuses in the Texas state higher education system and to major in "something standard" like communications.

But as academic fate would have it, Wallis, 23, learned that Brookhaven   2
Community College in the Dallas area offered a two-year degree in automotive technology. She discovered that the program was designed to do more than train grease monkeys for the corner service station. The course would not only enable her to tinker with cars but would provide the education base for a management position in the auto industry. Moreover, students were required to take a mixture of technology and traditional liberal arts courses so that they could, if they wished, transfer to a four-year school. The clincher: Each student would be given a paid internship and after graduation would be guaranteed a job at a local auto dealership.

$60,000 plus. Today, five years later, Wallis laughs at the idea that a   3
vocational degree is either demeaning or inevitably leads to a low-paid, dead end job. Now a sales manager for Sewell Cadillac in Dallas, she explains that "a few years out of school, it's nothing for graduates of the auto program to pull down $60,000 a year." Brookhaven officials add that

some graduates earn well in excess of that figure. Wallis herself sees a clear path ahead. She plans to take advantage of her employer's offer to pay for furthering her education and then move upward: "The sky's the limit for me."

Wallis's success is one answer to snobbish critics who demean com- 4 munity college education as "merely vocational training." At a time when graduates of academically "pure" programs at four-year colleges are finding appropriate jobs harder and harder to come by, it is not surprising that occupation-oriented degrees and certificates awarded by the nation's more than 1,200 community colleges are becoming increasingly attractive to students. While the two-year programs may lack cachet, for many they often offer something far more important: guaranteed jobs. Most community colleges have agreements with local businesses that assure jobs for graduates of many programs, particularly those in leading-edge fields such as computer technology, health care, and environmental science. Little wonder that the overall number of students at community colleges has jumped 35 percent, from 4.7 million in 1985 to 6.4 million in 1992.

Vocational programs perhaps have been most successful in Cheri 5 Wallis's home state of Texas, where the 70 community colleges have cooperative arrangements with more than 6,500 companies and administer 90 percent of the training and retraining programs for the state's corporations. And while enrollment at public universities in Texas has grown only 14 percent since 1985, the number of students opting for community and technical colleges has jumped 36 percent. In Dallas, the state's largest community college district, some 55,000 students can choose from among more than 100 technical and career programs, ranging from graphic arts to robotics technology. Says Bill Wenrich, chancellor of the district: "There's hardly a vocational program we offer that doesn't feed into a four-year degree, should a student wish to continue his or her education at any point down the road."

William Long went the other way: from a four-year to a two-year school. 6 At the end of his sophomore year at Southern Methodist University in Dallas, the 20-year-old native of nearby Garland gave up a full $65,000 scholarship to enroll at Eastfield Community College in the Dallas suburb of Mesquite. "I was studying sports medicine and kept hearing all kinds of horror stories about people not finding work or finding only lousy jobs," recalls Long, who was also impressed by the example of his father. The elder Long had quit truck driving and had earned degrees in digital electronics and telecommunications from the Eastfield campus in 1992.

Immediately after graduation, William's dad was hired by Northern 7 Telecom in nearby Richardson and just over a year later promoted to the job level of graduates of four-year colleges. With the elder Long's experience in mind, William decided to take a few courses himself at Eastfield while still at SMU. After completing four Eastfield courses, he notified SMU that he would not return for his junior year. Long hopes to earn his degree from Eastfield in 1995 and to begin working alongside his father at Northern Telecom. "Some of my friends thought I was crazy," says Long, "but now many have no idea how they're going to find a job when they graduate."

Even though Kelly Scott did have a job when she graduated in 1987   8 from Ohio's Wittenberg University with a degree in philosophy, she found herself unemployed after being caught in an IBM downsizing. After deciding not to risk more downsizing at a large corporation, Kelly opted to fulfill a lifelong desire: She would become a chef. Discouraged in the past by the $25,000 cost of a prominent culinary institute in which she was interested, she discovered the famous apprenticeship program for chefs at the El Centro Community College in Dallas, where her parents had settled. Today, Scott, 29, works full time as an apprentice cook at the Omni Mandalay Hotel in the Dallas suburb of Las Colinas and in her spare time takes courses at El Centro—paid for by her employer—in subjects like business management and nutrition. "What I'm learning will enable me to open my own restaurant one day," says Scott. "That's my dream."

With success stories like these in mind, community colleges, a distinc-   9 tively American innovation in higher education, are the focus of several new pieces of federal legislation designed to train and retrain the work force. The measures include the School-to-Work Opportunities Act, passed in May [1994], which encourages partnerships among high schools, community colleges, and businesses to prepare students for quality jobs that do not require four-year degrees. The Omnibus Reemployment Act of 1994, parts of which have already received funding, will aid community college programs in retraining displaced workers. "For too many years, American society has been splitting people according to whether or not they hold a B.A.," says Labor Secretary Robert Reich. "Today, a B.A. cannot and should not be the parchment that divides winners from losers."

Questions About the Reading

1. What is the main idea of the article?
2. Which liberal arts courses do you think would be included in Cheri Wallis's automotive program?

3. Why did William Long transfer from a four-year to a two-year college? Do you think he made a wise long-range decision? Why?
4. What courses is Kelly Scott taking in addition to those included in her culinary program? Why?

Thinking Critically

1. What liberal arts courses do you think would be included in the vocational/technical programs taken by the students mentioned in the article?
2. What skills and competencies do you think Wallis needs as a sales manager for a Cadillac agency?
3. What liberal arts courses do you think would be relevant to William Long's electronics/telecommunications program?
4. What skills and competencies do you think Scott will need to own and operate her own restaurant?

Writing Assignments

1. In your journal, list the advantages and disadvantages of liberal arts and vocational/technical education paths.
2. Working with several classmates, discuss and combine your journal lists and write a formal report in which you discuss the advantages and disadvantages of liberal arts and vocational/technical paths. Include a title page, table of contents, and abstract with your report.

Cooperative Education: Learn More, Earn More, Prepare for the Workplace

Matthew Mariani

In this article from the Occupational Outlook Quarterly, *Matthew Mariani explains the cooperative education process and provides some tables of earnings for associate degree and bachelor degree students.*

Before You Read

What are the advantages of a cooperative education path? What do you think are the disadvantages?

Words to Know

résumé   account or summary of a person's education and work

stipend   payment for services

Studies show that few people learn to drive a car without getting behind the wheel. Imagine a nonmotorist just reading a book about driving and then zooming off to Albuquerque. That would be hitting the highway the hard way. 1

As it happens, clever college students also learn by doing, and, in the United States, about a quarter of a million of them choose cooperative education. Co-op jump starts classroom study by alternating it with periods of work. Students gain hands-on experience related to their major field of study and career goals by following a school-approved plan. 2

Co-oping has many benefits. It helps students map out a career path. The money they earn as co-op employees pays some of their academic tolls along that path. After graduation, their work experience revs up a résumé and may lead them to permanent employment. . . . 3

Orientation

To get things rolling, co-op coordinators often orient students to the program in one session. Like cars, co-op programs have their own custom features, so coordinators cover the particulars about their school, as well as the basics. 4

Students first learn the magic number for cooperative education. It's the number three, because co-op depends on a partnership between three players: Student, college (represented by the coordinator), and co-op employers who hire students for work lasting from 2 to 6 months.

The scheduling of this work varies at the 900 or so U.S. colleges offering co-op. Not all schools alternate between separate periods of work and study. Some have students go to class in the morning and work in the afternoon. Community colleges most often do this. Certain colleges mix the two modes of scheduling.

Programs leading to an associate's degree take at least 2 years. For a bachelor's degree, schools offer 4- or 5-year co-op programs. The total time spent on co-op work ranges from 6 months to 2 years, depending on the degree and the school. Some colleges grant academic credit for the work experience.

Get Ready, Get Set

Co-op gives students a headstart on learning job search skills. Students write résumés and then interview with employers to compete for available co-op positions. . . .

The timing and mode of job search training differs from one program to another. Students can't wait too long to polish their résumés and interviewing skills, though, because they need to start work quickly. Two-year schools may allow students to go to work after only one term of study. In bachelor's programs, co-op work may begin after a year or two in the classroom and sometimes sooner. . . .

Earnings vary by major. Technical majors, like computer science, command more money than nontechnical ones in liberal arts, social sciences, or humanities. Some jobs pay only a small stipend or nothing at all. These positions are typically in less technical areas, like human services.

In some cases, students do earn enough to pay their own way. Those who attend a community college with low tuition or opt for a very technical major like engineering technology might manage fine. Someone pursuing a bachelor's degree in sociology at a costly liberal arts school, however, might afford to buy little more with co-op earnings than books and a few days worth of tuition. Most students will find themselves someplace in between these two examples.

National data on co-op earnings are not available, but a Wayne State University survey sent to co-op schools in nine midwestern states offers a useful measure. The accompanying tables show initial and final earnings for co-op employees by major. . . .

Table 1 Median Monthly Salaries of Co-op Employees at the Associate's Degree Level in the Midwest by Major, 1993[1]

	MEDIAN MONTHLY SALARY	
Major	Starting	Ending
Business		
All business	$1,183	$1,320
Accounting	1,204	1,364
Banking and finance	1,360	1,440
Secretarial sciences	1,126	1,216
Business, management, agribusiness	1,161	1,320
Data processing	1,204	1,290
Hospitality and hotel and food management	1,226	1,469
Sales, marketing, and merchandising	1,161	1,400
Engineering and related		
All engineering and related	1,275	1,429
Automotive services	1,060	1,188
Civil and construction	1,204	1,420
Drafting and design	1,202	1,256
Electrical and electronic	1,440	1,591
Mechanical and mechanics	1,371	1,548
Other		
Graphics and commercial art	1,161	1,292
Medical, nursing, and related	1,393	1,613
Criminal justice and law enforcement	1,591	2,000

1 The survey included schools in Illinois, Indiana, Iowa, Kentucky, Michigan, Minnesota, Missouri, Ohio, and Wisconsin.

Source: 1993 Cooperative Education Student Employee Salary & Benefits Survey (Midwest Region), Wayne State University.

Table 2 Median Monthly Salaries of Co-op Employees at the Bachelor's Degree Level in the Midwest by Major, 1993[1]

Major	MEDIAN MONTHLY SALARY	
	Starting	Ending
Business		
All business	$1,337	$1,621
Accounting	1,360	1,640
Banking and finance	1,380	1,562
Management	1,238	1,548
Management information systems	1,396	1,793
Marketing	1,290	1,548
Humanities and social sciences		
All humanities and social sciences	1,069	1,443
Humanities	1,079	1,548
Social sciences	1,061	1,364
Sciences		
All sciences	1,321	1,633
Agriculture	1,336	1,290
Biology	1,413	1,800
Computer science	1,406	1,832
Chemistry	1,462	2,040
Mathematics	1,400	1,829
Physics	1,400	1,850
Engineering		
All engineering	1,562	1,988
Chemical	1,664	2,193
Civil	1,400	1,672
Electrical, electronic, and computer	1,624	2,064
Industrial	1,575	2,000
Mechanical	1,585	2,039
Engineering technology (all types)	1,396	1,735
Other		
Architecture	1,119	1,473
Economics	1,400	1,470
Nursing and allied health	1,400	1,708
Criminal justice	1,400	1,500

[1] The survey included schools in Illinois, Indiana, Iowa, Kentucky, Michigan, Minnesota, Missouri, Ohio, and Wisconsin.
Source: 1993 Cooperative Education Student Employee Salary & Benefits Survey (Midwest Region), Wayne State University.

Questions About the Reading

1. How many students in the United States choose cooperative education?
2. According to the writer, what are the benefits of cooperative education?
3. What do students generally learn in an orientation to cooperative education?
4. Who are the persons involved in the cooperative education partnership?
5. What are the job search skills generally included in cooperative education?

Thinking Critically

1. Would cooperative education satisfy your deep interests?
2. Which of the skills and competencies required in your anticipated career would a cooperative education provide?
3. What liberal arts courses do you think would be included in a cooperative education program?

Writing Assignments

1. Using the tables included in the article, develop a table showing the four majors at the associate and bachelor degree levels with the highest ending salaries.
2. Working with classmates, develop a table identifying the English, mathematics, science, computer, and educational requirements (associate, bachelor, or graduate degree) for at least three cooperative education programs.

Find Work That You Love

Barbara Moses

Barbara Moses is a career-management consultant. In this excerpt from her book Career Intelligence: 12 New Rules for Career Success, *she tells us that we should assess our own skills and strengths when deciding on a career and provides us with rules for success in our chosen careers.*

Before You Read

What kind of work do you love? Do you think the work you love will provide you with the kind of life you desire?

Words to Know

aptitudes   abilities, skills
attributes   qualities, characteristics
ensuring   guaranteeing
indulgence   satisfaction
naïve   innocent
portfolio   collection, list

... "Do what you love." "Follow your bliss." We have all heard this type 1
of apparently impractical advice for job seekers. But this advice is actually very practical. All things being equal, the chances are that you will do better and be happier doing work that you love than work to which you are indifferent—or actively dislike.

But finding work that you love is not as blissfully easy as the peppy 2
self-help books might suggest. You may have to make considerable sacrifices and difficult trade-offs, but becoming an activist in your career means you will be in a position to make choices. If you never even look for the work you love, your life will be poorer for it.

Knowing what you love starts with **knowing what is important to** 3
you. Knowing your personal priorities and values is crucial in ensuring your career satisfaction. ...

Be Who You Are

Marian, a successful senior manager, recently quit her job. Warm and expressive with her friends and family, she found herself becoming increasingly "cold and hard" to survive in an unrelentingly tough corporate en- 4

53

vironment. "It was getting to the point where I no longer recognized myself. I had to get out of there or go crazy," she said.

Don't try to be something you're not. Be who you are—your authentic   5
self. Find an organizational culture that reflects your personal needs and values, an environment that allows you to be you. You'll be happier. And in the long run, you'll probably be more successful.

One study looked at the characteristics of 55 successful women execu-   6
tives who held powerful positions in major American corporations. One of the most striking things they had in common was their honesty and directness. They didn't pretend to be something they weren't. They expressed their own individuality. They weren't defensive or "political." And their careers flourished.

Being who you are may mean **refusing to "worship the new market**   7
god." Five years ago, you would routinely hear parents make comments about their children such as, "I don't really care what they decide to do as long as they're happy." I don't hear anyone make this comment today. It's almost as if the stakes have become so high that people feel that happiness as an end in itself is an indulgence one can ill afford. Never before has people's measure of worth and "fitness" been so intimately tied to their economic viability.

People turn themselves inside out to fit into positions that are a funda-   8
mentally awful match with their skills, interests, and values because they are so terrified of being without a job. They make career choices on the basis of how it will look on their résumé. They work excessive hours at the expense of their health, their children, and their personal relationships.

At some point, we have to step back and refuse to worship blindly at   9
the altar of the market god—to do what we want to do rather than contorting ourselves into whatever shape the market currently happens to demand.

Instead, we must learn to **play to our strengths.** Each of us brings to   10
the table a unique set of skills and attributes that describe who we are and how we can add value. When we stray too far from these core strengths, we invite trouble.

Increasingly, I see people worrying because their organization has de-   11
cided that in order for them to be successful they have to possess certain attributes and competencies. For example, they need to "be creative," to "have good leadership skills," or to "be able to withstand enormous pressure." In evaluating themselves against these competencies, people often identify one or two areas where they are not as strong, and ask: "How can I become more creative? How can I be a better leader? How can I become more effective under pressure? What does it mean if I have a liability or weakness in a particular area?"

Self-help books and motivational courses would have us believe that 12 we can be whatever we want to be, if we only try hard enough. I think this is psychologically naïve. We are all different, and each of us has our own unique portfolio of strengths and aptitudes.

The 12 New Rules for Career Success

It is not enough to know what the new emerging careers are for building 13 a successful future for yourself. The job market isn't that stable anyway. The workplace has changed, and the rules of career success have changed along with it.

1. Ensure Your Marketability

Ben, 45, was a middle manager in a company that eradicated its entire 14 middle-management ranks. It took him 18 months to find another job— and two years to recover emotionally. Now, Ben says, "Every six months I take out my résumé, and if I can't think of one thing I've accomplished that I can add, I know that I've been slacking off."

It may no longer be realistic to believe that job security exists anywhere 15 anymore. But you can have security in the marketability of your skills. To make yourself marketable:

- Think of everyone you work for as a client rather than a boss.
- Know your product: yourself and the skills you have to offer, your assets, strengths, potential liabilities, and how you can add value to an employer or client.
- Know your market: both current and prospective clients.

2. Think Globally

Philip, a Toronto architect, struggled for a few years in what he described 16 as a dying profession. "They're no longer building office towers," he complained. "They were all done in the 1980s." But he secured a new livelihood by going online and networking to find new clients as far away as Saudi Arabia. Philip still lives in Toronto but travels back and forth to the Middle East.

Today's technology allows you to work anywhere, anytime. And in a 17 global economy, you may have to. In the borderless work world, where the entire world is a potential market, the ability to speak other languages and be comfortable with other cultures will be crucial. Globalization means an expansion of work opportunities, making you less reliant on the local economy. And living and working internationally helps you gain richer concepts not only in the mechanics of business, but also in the principles of life and work. As organizations increasingly move into new international markets, they will be looking for individuals who can adapt readily to other cultures.

3. Communicate Powerfully, Persuasively, and Unconventionally

Adrienne is an international art dealer who is now selling much of her art 18 on the Internet rather than through face-to-face communication; she has had to learn a completely new set of communication skills. In the past, she would build relationships and establish credibility with people over time through "schmoozing," charm, and professional expertise. To do the same thing online, she says, "I had to learn to use the written word the way I speak. I had to learn how to become an evocative writer—to charm, to talk about the feeling of a picture in a few powerful and suggestive words."

People with finely honed communication skills have always been val- 19 ued, but advances in telecommunications, geographically dispersed project work, and everyone's information overload mean that efficient and effective communication is needed more than ever. You must be able to:

- Quickly capture your listener's attention and get your message across.
- Use words to paint a picture, tell a story, make information vivid.
- Write clearly, persuasively, and with impact.
- Zero in on key concepts and translate them appropriately for your listener's requirements.

4. Keep on Learning

With constantly changing work and skill requirements, "lifelong learn- 20 ing" will be more than just a catchphrase. It will be a necessity. Rules of lifelong learning include:

- Stay current in your own field, and continue to develop skills and knowledge outside it.
- Take courses, read books and journals, develop and practice new skills.
- Look at periods of full-time education between periods of work not as "time off," but as smart career moves preparing you for the future.

When considering learning, don't confine yourself to traditional insti- 21
tutions or modes of learning. Perhaps the most important learning "event"
of recent years has been the number of people who have become computer literate—something achieved almost exclusively outside the traditional classroom.

As more and more educational institutes are going online, offering di- 22
verse learning experiences over the Internet (including graduate degrees),
it will be much easier to meet the need for lifelong learning.

5. Understand Business Trends

I am always amazed at how many people have only the narrowest knowl- 23
edge of specific trends in their profession and even less knowledge of
broader business trends—whether economic, demographic, or cultural. I
routinely ask people, "What international trends will affect your business?" and "Globally, what is your major source of competition?" Even
among senior managers, only a handful of people say they are as well
informed as they should be.

Test yourself: Do you regularly read the business section of your news- 24
paper? Can you identify three trends that will have significant impact on
your industry in the next five years? Do you know what new technologies might shape your industry in the next five years? Do you know what
the potential threats are to your industry or profession?

In a very complex and rapidly changing work world, it is crucial to be 25
aware of key trends in business, society, and politics. Not having the time
to keep up simply doesn't cut it as an excuse. Read the business press or
keep current through electronic media and keep track of the fast-
changing economic and social landscape. Understand the competitive environment. Get information from a variety of sources and maintain an
independent and critical perspective.

6. Prepare for Areas of Competence, Not Jobs

Recently someone suggested computer animation as a possible future 26
career for Barry, a teenager with storytelling, graphics, and media abilities. Barry replied, "The work I choose now might not even exist by the
time I'm old enough to do it. Or if it does exist, the technology may have
changed to require completely different skills."

Intuitively, Barry understood a key maxim of the new economy: Don't 27
prepare for jobs, prepare for areas of competence. Like many of yesterday's
jobs that have now vanished, the "hot jobs" of today may not exist tomorrow.

It is important, then, to think of roles, not jobs. You may have a single 28
job title but many, many roles: leader, change agent, coach, problem solver,
troubleshooter, team builder, consensus builder, mentor, facilitator, and
so on. Think also of marketable skills that are independent of your technical abilities, such as resilient, resourceful, opportunity seeking, time
urgent, market driven, high-impact risk taker, and insatiable learner. These
are the self-management attributes and skills that employers are looking
for and that will determine your future success in the new economy.

7. Look to the Future

You can't rely on the accuracy of long-term occupational projections, nor 29
should you try to make career choices based on what kind of work you
think will be "hot," rather than what you are best suited to do. But it is
still helpful to monitor demographic, economic, and cultural trends.

Based on current trends, here are some of the fields that should be 30
fairly buoyant:

- **Medicine.** Many of the new openings will be at the lower end of
  the scale (e.g., home care workers and nursing assistants), but there
  will also be openings for occupational and physical therapists,
  pharmacists, and radiologists, as well as specialties that will help
  keep an aging population active and youthful looking: plastic surgery, for instance.
- **Education.** School boards are cutting back on jobs for teachers,
  but educators and entrepreneurs alike will be able to profit from
  the growth of private tutoring services and centers. . . .
- **Edutainment.** The growth of electronic media and the emphasis
  on lifelong learning add up to tremendous opportunities for people
  who can combine the excitement of computer graphics and
  animation with educational content—everyone from the entrepreneurs who package and market the products to computer program-
  mers, graphic artists, animators, and educators.

Other "hot" areas include recreation, the environment, biotechnology, 31
pharmaceuticals, communications, computers, and personal services of
all kinds.

8. Build Financial Independence

When your finances are in good shape, you can make career decisions based 32
on what is really important to you. A financial planner can help you take
steps toward financial independence. Most recommend that you save about
10% of your pretax income and keep six months' salary in the bank.

Rethink your relationship to money: Does all the stuff you buy con- 33
tribute to your happiness? If not, could you give up buying it? You might
take a lesson from the "voluntary simplicity" movement, in which people
have actively decided to pursue a life outside the continual push to "buy,
spend, consume." What do you really need?

9. Think Lattice, Not Ladders

Corporate downsizing and flattened hierarchies have carved out half the 34
rungs in the traditional career ladder. Now, the career ladder is more like
a lattice: You may have to move sideways before you can move up.

In a lattice, everything is connected. Each step will take you some- 35
where, though sometimes in unpredictable directions. You must measure
progress in new ways. Each new work assignment should contribute to
your portfolio of skills, in increasing both your breadth and depth, while
you stay motivated and challenged.

Be creative in seeking out new opportunities. When 42-year-old Ira 36
was told that he would never make partner at his accounting firm, he
looked for opportunities not only to keep himself challenged, but also to
maintain his visibility and value to the firm. Every two years or so, Ira
takes on a high-profile assignment, thus making himself an indispens-
able contributor to the firm.

If you're feeling stuck in your current role, consider the possibilities 37
for job enrichment: a lateral move into a new work assignment that offers
opportunities for learning and development, opportunities to mentor
younger staff, participation in task forces, and interesting educational
programs.

Track your career progress by your work, not your level. Judge your 38
progress by the depth of content of your work, its importance to the organization and to customers, and whether you are still learning and having fun.

10. Be a Generalist with a Specialty or a Specialist Who's a Generalist

Will you be better off in the future as a specialist or as a generalist? The 39
answer is, Both. You need to have strong enough specialist skills to get
you in the door—something that makes you unique and puts you in a
position to add value to a client. But that is no longer enough.

You also need to be able to use those specialist skills in high-pressure 40
environments and in teams of people from different disciplines. You also
need to be able to organize your work, manage your time, keep a budget,

and sell a project. So the question is not so much one of either/or, but one of degree. Should you be *more* of a specialist or *more* of a generalist?

If you prefer to specialize, conduct a searching self-assessment to make 41 sure you have what it takes to rise to the top of your profession. Take an equally careful look at market conditions to make sure that you are investing your career assets in an in-demand specialty. Stay on top of the newest trends and information in your profession. And don't give up on your general skills.

11. Be a Ruthless Time Manager

We are working in a world where fast enough never is and where speed 42 is prized above all else. With so many demands on us, it's crucial to be ruthless in managing time.

Evaluate every time commitment. Are you doing something because it 43 needs to be done or because it's there? What are you not doing that may be more important? Become vigilant in saying "no" to excessive work demands. Know your limitations. Work strategically rather than just staying busy. If you are working excessively long hours over an extended period of time, you may lose productivity.

Set priorities, including personal priorities. Use the weekend to refresh 44 yourself—turn off the cell phone. Go someplace where you can't be reached.

12. Be Kind to Yourself

Instead of beating yourself up over things that didn't work out, remind 45 yourself of your successes. Celebrate them!

Set realistic expectations of what's doable. Learn to live with the best 46 you can do at this point, to live with less-than-perfect. Congratulate yourself on your successes. When you've done a good job, pat yourself on the back. Regularly keep track of your successes, no matter how apparently small, and take credit where it's due. Above all, be kind to yourself.

Questions About the Reading

1. What advice does the writer give for finding work you love?
2. What does the writer mean by "ensure your marketability"?
3. According to the writer, what communication skills do you need for career success?

4. What does the writer mean by "Be a Generalist with a Specialty or a Specialist Who's a Generalist"?

Thinking Critically

1. What do you think would be the effect on the country if everyone decided to do only work that they love?
2. What are the technical and communication skills needed in the career you are considering?
3. How will the growing global economy affect the career you are considering?

Writing Assignments

1. In your journal, develop a portfolio of your strengths and aptitudes.
2. Write an abstract of "The 12 New Rules for Career Success" section of the article.
3. Working with classmates and using the help-wanted ads in your local newspaper, determine the jobs for which there are the most openings. Using the information in the ads, your school's career guidance resources, and calls to some of the ads, find out what technical and communication skills are needed for the jobs. Write a formal report explaining the skills required and comparing the requirements to the curriculum of your school that would prepare you for the job. Include a title page, table of contents, and abstract with the report.

3

Family and Gender Issues

NO MATTER WHAT career you choose, there will be times when you have to make choices between the demands of your work and the needs of your family. Balancing career and family life becomes even more complex when children are involved. Cokie Roberts shares her own experiences as wife, mother, reporter, writer, and television commentator in "A Woman's Place" and tells us that a woman's role is different at different times and in different places.

When children are part of the decision-making process, perhaps the father or the mother will decide to stay home. In "Women Who Stay at Home and Love It!" four women share their decisions to stay home with their children. Although a growing number of men have made that same decision, Joan K. Peters raises the issue of fathers being reluctant to take even family-leave time away from work in "Being There: The Father Quandary."

The stress for women who choose to combine marriage, family, and career has been well documented and acknowledged. In "What Today's Fathers Want," James A. Levine and Todd L. Pittinsky show us that men suffer from the same stresses and conflicts between work and family as women do.

Combining education, career, and family life is also difficult. In "Still Seeking the Perfect Balance," Elizabeth McGuire tells us how she and her husband are working out the problem of balancing education, career, and family.

Business Letters

In this chapter you will be asked to write a letter. Suppose, for example, that you want to answer the following advertisement for a job.

COLLEGE STUDENTS
Benefits a cut above. Special office
project. Top $$$$$$$. Get in on the
job experience.
ADDRESS QUERIES TO:
MS. J. C. WILLIAMS
OFFICE SERVICES
P.O. BOX 5050
CLEVELAND, OHIO 44101

Because there is little information in the ad about the work or the business involved, you want—and are entitled to—more information about the job, its requirements, and its location. Your letter requesting information might look like this:

[Letterhead containing your name and address]

[Phone number, fax number, e-mail address—

optional]

[Date]

Ms. J. C. Williams

Office Services

P.O. Box 5050   Inside address

Cleveland, Ohio 44101

Dear Ms. Williams: Salutation

I am interested in the position you advertised in

[name of newspaper] of [date] for "College

Students." I am a [year] in college, majoring in   Body

[your major]. I have completed [math, English,

science, computer] courses.

I would appreciate it if you would advise me by

[date] about the specific skills required for the   Body

project and the nature and location of the work.

Yours truly,   Complimentary
                                                          close

[Name]

[Signature]

Notice that the letter is brief but provides the advertiser with the student's relevant educational information and with the specific information that the student wants. Notice, too, the analysis of the parts of the letter in the right margin.

The example letter is written in block style; that is, the first word of each paragraph is not indented and there is a line of space between the paragraphs. Business letters are generally written in block style, but if you prefer, the first word of each paragraph may be indented.

The letter should be enclosed in a business-size $9^1/_2 \times 4^1/_8$-inch envelope and should be addressed as follows:

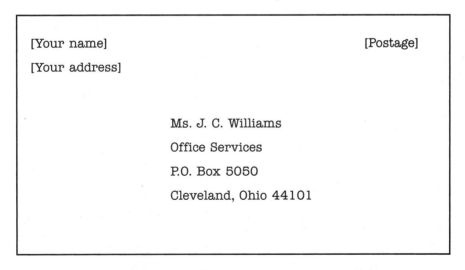

In your work you may need to write letters asking for information, ordering materials, selling your company's product, or responding to a customer's request or complaint. In addition to following the organization of the example letter above, the content of any business letter should be clear, specific, and brief. Tell your reader exactly what you are writing about or what it is you want. Tell your reader in as few words as possible and make your purpose clear and specific.

Suppose, for example, that you work for the ABC Towel Company. You need to order binding for the towels your company manufactures and want to obtain prices from several companies. Your letter, which could be duplicated for each binding manufacturer you want to query, might look like the following example:

ABC TOWEL COMPANY

3694 ROBERTS STREET

HARTFORD, CONNECTICUT

26001

December 1, 2000

Mr. William L. Jackson

Vice President, Sales

Fletcher Binding Manufacturing Company

P.O. Box 66520

Atlanta, Georgia 31201

Dear Mr. Jackson:

I would appreciate it if you would provide me with price quotations for the following binding materials:

Catalog number	Amount	Size	Color/fabric
FB680	5,000 yds.	$1/_2$ inch	White cotton
FB223	3,000 yds.	1 inch	White 60/40 cotton/polyester
FB145	2,000 yds	1 inch	Green cotton
FB421	2,000 yds	$1/_2$ inch	Green 60/40 cotton/polyester

Thank you for sending this information to me either by e-mail or fax by December 12. My e-mail is jcwilson@abctowel.com.

My fax number is 1-912-358-5015.

Yours truly,

John C. Wilson

Purchasing Manager

A Woman's Place

Cokie Roberts

Cokie Roberts is well known as a White House reporter, writer, and co-host of ABC's Sunday morning This Week *show. In this chapter from her book* We Are Our Mother's Daughters, *she tells us that women's role as nurturer to family and friends means their place is different at different times and in different places.*

Before You Read

What is your opinion of women who work outside the home when they have children?

Words to Know

stigma   stain, mark of disgrace or reproach
transcend   go beyond, surpass
vicious   unruly, malicious, spiteful

"**A** woman's place is in the House . . . and in the Senate," the T-shirts and   1
buttons proclaim at women's political events. "A Woman's Place Is in Uniform," trumpets a book about women in the military. "A woman's place is at the typewriter," declared *Fortune* magazine back in 1935. That was convenient for the economy and so it was decreed. A few years later a woman's place was in the factory or in the nursing corps because that was essential for the war effort. Then a woman's place was in the home. And now? A woman's place is anywhere she wants it to be. Fine, but who's taking care of the children? That's the question that keeps us roiled up over this issue.

Recently the country got all in a snit over the case of a baby apparently   2
killed by his baby-sitter in Boston. Were people demanding the head of the baby-sitter? No, quite the contrary, it was the mother who came in for abuse by the radio callers and the editorial writers. She went to work three days a week, coming home at lunchtime to breast-feed, even though her husband had a perfectly good job. What kind of mother was she? Obviously, a selfish, greedy one who was willing to leave her children in the care of an inexperienced young woman. Wait a minute. Suppose she had gone out at night with her husband and left the babies with a teen-ager? What then? And didn't society just direct thousands of mothers to

leave their children in another's care by requiring that welfare mothers go to work? Could we make up our minds here, please?

No, probably not, because we're still confused about this issue of a 3 woman's place. We're confused because we know that no matter what else a woman is doing, she's also caretaking and we worry that a woman "out at work" might leave someone, especially her children, without care. That's what's at the heart of this sometimes vicious debate. Sure, a lot of other, much less noble, attitudes also underlie these arguments. Plenty of people still think that women are just plain uppity and they see a woman's place as someplace to put her. But I think it's the question of the children, and now old people as well, that truly troubles us. And women with children often find whatever choice they make uncomfortable.

That wasn't always true. For most of human history men and women 4 worked together in the same place and each one's work complemented the other's. No one thought the farmer's job was more important than the farm wife's. Neither could manage without the other. Teenage relatives often moved in to help care for the children, to protect them from household hazards like open fires while the busy mother made the soap and the candles, spun the cloth, pieced together the clothes, fixed the food. Women gathered together to help with large chores, and visited as they worked. They also congregated to attend to births and deaths, taking comfort from each other's company.

. . . It was the industrial revolution that changed everything. Men went 5 out to work for wages, and they were paid for the hours they put in, not the tasks they completed. . . . Suddenly, what women did at home lost its value because there was no paycheck attached. Repetitive housework replaced home manufacture as women's crafts moved into assembly-line production. And that's what we've been struggling with ever since. Doing work that is economically rewarded and socially recognized means leaving home. That could change with the information revolution, as machines make it possible to work just about anywhere. But I think it's unlikely to alter the fact that women aren't paid for their jobs as nurturers, and it still leaves women at home isolated from other women.

It's important, I think, for young women today to understand that they 6 are not the first generation to deal with these questions. . . . But knowing that you're not the first to have to cope with a problem doesn't necessarily make solving it any easier. And for reasons that I don't fully understand, women make each other's lives harder by trying to impose their own choices on their sisters. Again, it's important to be clear eyed here that we are talking only about women privileged enough to have choices. If society makes some statement about mothers and children, it should relate to all mothers and children.

Over the last forty years, I've watched this argument go full circle. 7
When I was in high school and college, my friends' mothers did not work,
and there was definitely a stigma attached to female employment. My
own mother escaped it because she worked for and with my father, which
was acceptable. Keep in mind, this was not long after World War II, when
there was an organized effort to get women out of the workplace. . . .

With the advent of modern feminism, it was women at home who were 8
looked down upon by their fellow females. What were they doing with
their educations? How could they allow themselves to be so dependent
on a male? Didn't they know he could up and leave them penniless at
any moment? The women's movement gave lip service to the concept of
choice, but didn't mean it. The strong message: Women, to have any worth,
you must go to work, show that you are just like a man.

Now, there's a swing back to stigmatizing the at-work woman if she is 9
a mother. Some of these critiques are ridiculous. I remember reading one
in our local newspaper where the author opined that a working mother
wouldn't be able to bake with the children, hand down the cookie recipes
from generation to generation. I thought of my cabinet full of cookie cutters—Christmas cookie cutters, Hanukkah cookie cutters, Valentine cookie
cutters, Halloween cookie cutters—and the hours I have put in rolling
the dough, overseeing the decoration ("No, you can't dump a whole bottle
of sprinkles on one cookie") and all I could do was laugh. Then I got
angry. Who was she to question my choices? And why did she want to?
To validate her own.

Obviously, there's good reason to be concerned about children and if 10
this country's ready to have a serious conversation about children, I'm
all for it. But that conversation goes to far more fundamental questions
than how some middle- and upper-middle-class women spend a few years
of their lives. Let's talk about children in danger from their parents and
their neighborhoods, children who are hungry, children who can't get
educated in the public schools, children whose parents use them as pawns
in domestic wars, children who are lonely, children who have no hope
for their futures, if we truly want to concern ourselves with America's
kids. Children who have two parents married to each other and who care
enough about them to worry about work versus home are already well
ahead of the game. I don't mean to belittle the difficulty in making those
choices, I'm just trying to put them in perspective.

Women would do well to take the long view in making personal deci- 11
sions, as we always have. The number of years we have children at home,
particularly preschool children, is few. The number of years available to
move ahead in the work force is many, assuming we live full lifespans.
Putting career on the back, or at least the middle, burner in the years

children are small makes a lot of sense to me. That doesn't necessarily mean staying home full-time. For me, that would have been a disaster. I need to work for my spiritual and emotional well-being, and while that might not be admirable, it's true. In interim periods between jobs I've suffered genuine depression, and believe me, that's not good for the children. I was a better mother because I worked. . . .

That's not to say that there have never been times my family's suffered 12 because of my job. Of course there were. The kids still resent the long wait for dinner every night, the calls saying that we'd be home, and then the calls saying we'd be later than expected. I'm sure there were times that it would have been more comfortable and comforting for them if I had been home after school, times that it would have been helpful to them if I were available to drive them on errands or to see friends. As your kids get older they don't want you around most of the time, but when they want you, they want you. Unfortunately, there's no way to schedule those times, they just happen. You can schedule the things you know about, and there Steven and I had a pretty good track record. We were there for everything—the adjustments to new schools, the activities, the performances, and I was very involved in the PTAs over the years. . . .

So yes, there were times that my work got in the way of my family. 13 And there were times when my family got in the way of my work. It will continue to do so. Children might be our first responsibility but let's not kid ourselves, women care for the whole family, which includes the family of friends. A few years ago the *New York Times* published a poll which revealed that two thirds of all women aged eighteen to fifty-five work outside the home, half said they provided at least half the family income, and almost 20 percent were the sole providers. Regardless of job, 90 percent said they were the principle caretakers for their families. I guess the other 10 percent just haven't figured it out yet. And this nurturing goes on forever. My thirtieth college reunion class book includes this entry: "George's parents are still in good health and maintain active lives. We think it is remarkable that his 81-year-old father and 78-year-old mother look after George's 100-year-old grandmother who still lives alone in her Wisconsin farmhouse." . . .

Just a few weeks before she died at the age of ninety-seven, former 14 senator Margaret Chase Smith wrote an introduction to the book *Outstanding Women Members of Congress*. "'Where is the proper place of women?' is a question I have often been asked," she begins. "The quizzers have asked this question ambitiously, defiantly, hopefully—and just plain inquisitively. But it has been asked so many times in so many ways and by so many types of people that, of necessity, my answer has had to transcend the normal and understandable prejudice that a woman might have. My answer is short and simple—woman's proper place is everywhere.

Individually it is where the particular woman is happiest and best fit-ted—in the home as wives and mothers; in organized civic, business, and professional groups; in industry and business, both management and la-bor; and in government and politics. Generally, if there is any proper place for women today, it is that of alert and responsible citizens in the fullest sense of the word."

Because our communities and our country need us just as the children 15 do, the country requires the services of women soldiers and politicians and businesswomen and clubwomen and consumer and civil rights ac-tivists and women helping other women get off welfare and nurses and nuns. The country needs us to be sisters and aunts and friends and moth-ers and daughters and wives first in the literal sense, and then in the figurative one—sisters to society, caretakers. Women can complain for-ever about how our devotion to those roles is not remunerated, that soci-ety doesn't compensate us for our nurturing. And frankly, I don't think we'll ever solve that problem. If we want public recognition and financial reward we will continue to have to "do it all." But that's not such a ter-rible thing. One piece of advice for young women: don't worry about it so much. There are times when life's emotionally and physically exhaust-ing, and times when sleep deprivation seems likely to do you in, but you'll make it. Women are tough, we've managed to keep all the balls in the air for a very long time. . . .

So what is a woman's place? For most women it's many places, differ- 16 ent places at different times. For almost all women, it's the place of nurturer, whether for the planet or one small creature on it. We learned it from our mothers, both in word and in deed, we teach it to our daughters in the knowledge that they must carry on the culture and care for it. Even as they go forward into the next millennium, knowing things we never knew, they will be connected back to those women in Marathon, Greece. From that continuity they will derive the strength to make their place wherever they think it should be.

Questions About the Reading

1. What does the writer say is at the heart of the debate about women working outside the home?
2. What changed society's attitude toward women's work in their home? Why?
3. How did modern feminism affect working women's attitude toward women who stayed home?
4. What is society's attitude toward women who work when they have children?

Thinking Critically

1. Should the work of women—or men—who stay home with their children be recognized financially, perhaps by a tax deduction?
2. If all the women now working stayed home with their preschool children, what do you think would be the impact on the country and its economy?

Writing Assignments

1. Working with classmates, write an essay explaining whether women or men who stay home with their children should or should not receive financial recognition.
2. Working with classmates, write a formal report on the businesses and companies in your city that offer child care for their employees. Include the educational training provided, and construct tables for the hours of child care available and the costs for the different businesses and companies. Include a title page, table of contents, and abstract in your report. Assume your employer is the H. C. Wallace Company and you want the company to provide child care. Write a letter to transmit the report to the director of human resources.

Women Who Stay at Home and Love It!

Ebony *Magazine*

Many women—and men—choose to balance career, family, and child care, but the four women in this essay share their reasons for giving up their careers to stay at home with their children.

Before You Read

How do you plan to manage work, family, and child care responsibilities?

Words to Know

gratification   satisfaction, benefit
inflation   increase in prices, decrease in the value of money
privilege   advantage, favor

Do young girls still dream of sun-kissed kitchens with the smell of   1
fresh baked cookies and the sounds of their children's laughter drifting through the air? It's a safe bet that they do. But they dream of running major corporations with the sounds of stock market ticker tape clicking in the background, too.

There was a time when large numbers of women attended universities   2
and colleges primarily to find good husbands—i.e., men who earned enough money to support their families without their wives' help. Back then, married women, and society, expected wives to stay at home, nurture their families, and volunteer their time to civil, social, and community activities.

Then the Women's Movement—followed by high inflation and high   3
unemployment rates—ushered in new expectations. In the '90s, most young girls anticipate that they, like their mothers before them, will bring home the dough and bake it.

Nevertheless, there are women who stay at home and love it—and   4
they haven't been dragged there kicking and screaming in protest. They are home by choice, with the support of their husbands and despite societal expectations to the contrary.

Some of these women decided they would buck societal trends and   5
never work outside their homes. Some stay home to care for older or

disabled relatives. Most are full-time moms who stay at home with their children.

Among the women who have made these choices are Harvard University graduate Mattie McFadden-Lawson, Atty. Toi Treister, former office worker Talese Dickson, and former store clerk Bernadette Ramsey-Nolan. 6

Ramsey-Nolan, for example, and her husband, Mario Nolan, decided that once they began their family, she would stop working outside the home. For three years, the Chicago couple worked and saved in order to make their plans a reality. After Ramsey-Nolan's daughter Sarah was born a year ago, her husband, an Evanston, Ill., firefighter and paramedic, became his family's primary breadwinner. 7

"I really do feel fortunate," she says. "I feel it's a privilege to be a parent and to have the choice of staying at home with Sarah. A lot of people can't afford it. A lot of people don't enjoy it." 8

As a result of their decision, the Nolans maintain what some would consider a modest lifestyle. In order to save money, Ramsey-Nolan has covered their furniture with new slipcovers, and she sews some of her family's clothes. Their home isn't decked out in expensive furnishings and their walls aren't covered with elaborate artwork, but it is a warm and cozy abode brimming with good vibrations. 9

"It's just a joy watching her grow and teaching her different things," says Ramsey-Nolan, "and seeing new things that she does on her own." 10

Many women opt to stay at home because they want to be primarily responsible for molding their offspring. Other women recognize the benefits to their children but worry about permanently derailing their careers and losing sight of their hard-earned self-identity. But women can avoid these pitfalls, says Mattie McFadden-Lawson, if they remain focused on their personal goals and work on their self-development. 11

"Never just come home and sit," she advises. "Always have goals for yourself. If your goal is to be home, then fine—be the best mom or the best person you can be at home. If your goal is to be home until your children are a certain age and then return to work, that's fine. . . . If you're home and you have goals, you can still achieve them. It's just a function of staying on the path to accomplish them." 12

McFadden-Lawson talks a lot about delayed gratification, and she knows from experience what she's talking about. A graduate of Harvard's John F. Kennedy School of Government, she obtained a degree in public administration before her children were born. And she has worked on Capitol Hill and as an international investment banking officer in New York City. Now, she and her husband, Michael Lawson, live in Los Angeles with their two sons, Michael Jr., 10, and Jonathan, 5. An attorney, her husband is a partner in a law firm. 13

Explaining why she didn't return to work after Michael Jr. began school, 14
Mattie says: "I wanted to make sure that I was aware of what was going
on at his school and that I was actively involved with the school. I do-
nated my time there, and I was very much a part of his educational community."

Staying at home also has allowed McFadden-Lawson to volunteer some 15
of her time to the political campaigns of Rep. Maxine Waters (D-Calif). It
was work that connected her to the community and allowed her to have
control over her schedule. Finally, this year she realized a long-standing
personal goal when she enrolled in law school.

"I really feel that your destiny will take you where you need to be," 16
says McFadden-Lawson, "as long as you stay on the right path. But so
many of us get off the path because we give up. I have been very comfortable at home. I have not been one of those mothers who really dreaded it.
I got a chance to meet a lot of people. I got a chance to make a lot of
friends and to also get some great experience. It's been very worthwhile,
and I'm just very pleased with how everything turned out."

Talese and Victor Dickson of Olympia Fields, Ill., decided five years 17
ago that she would leave her 9-to-5 job and stay at home. With Dickson
away at work most of the day and her husband, a vice president of sales
for a major telecommunications corporation, frequently out of town, quality time with the children was often limited. And the couple did not like
the idea of entrusting the care of their children, Jacquea, 18, Makensi, 10,
and Darien, 11, to a stranger. Those feelings intensified two years ago
when Brianna was born. "You always hear about the day-care centers,"
says Dickson, "and we did not want them in an environment that may be
dangerous for them. I just strongly believe in giving my kids attention
and affection, and I didn't feel they would get that in any kind of daycare
service I may have put them in."

Like the Dicksons, Dana and Toi Treister have made financial sacri- 18
fices so that she can care for their offspring full-time. "I think you can tell
someone who's watching your kids how you want them raised," says Toi
Treister, "but when push comes to shove, you can't really reinforce that if
you're not there every day."

Treister, an attorney, gave up a full-time law practice to stay at home 19
with her 1-year-old daughter, Olivia, and her newborn daughter, Natalie.
She still works with a few clients from the family's home in Pasadena,
Calif., but her husband, Atty. Dana Treister, is the family's major breadwinner.

The couples featured here are among what many parents would con- 20
sider the fortunate few. Most mothers, and fathers for that matter, would
love to have at least one parent at home minding the kids. What working

couple hasn't wished for an at-home parent when faced with the choice of staying home with a sick child or going into the office to attend an important meeting?

Ten months ago, the Treisters were in a similar predicament. Both were 21 managing demanding careers, and they were placing the majority of Olivia's care in the hands of a nanny. "With commute time and everything," says Toi Treister, "we were looking at probably 15 hours a day— at least—that we weren't at home with Olivia. We had an in-home caretaker whom we trusted, but it just didn't seem right after a while."

Staying at home isn't a choice that every woman can—or wants to— 22 make. But many, like these women, love being at home and wouldn't have it any other way.

Questions About the Reading

1. How has the Nolans' life style been affected by Bernadette's decision to stay home with her daughter?
2. What advice does Mattie McFadden-Lawson have about deciding to stay at home? What is the goal she is now realizing?
3. Why did Talese Dickson decide to stay at home?
4. What is the career that Toi Treister gave up to stay at home? Why did she feel she should give it up?

Thinking Critically

1. Explain how you would use the basic thinking skills to raise children.
2. What are the personal qualities needed to manage a household and raise children?
3. What competencies are needed to manage a household and raise children?
4. What criteria might be used in deciding whether the mother or the father should stay home with the children?

Writing Assignments

1. Imagine that you have decided to leave your work and stay home with your children. Write a letter to your employer notifying him or her of your decision.
2. Working with classmates, write an essay explaining how the five competencies can be applied to managing a household and raising children.

Being There: The Father Quandary

Joan K. Peters

Although the recently passed Family and Medical Leave Act provides parental leave from work for the birth of a child, men are reluctant to take the time. Joan K. Peters tells us that shared parenting is necessary when both parents work and is important to their marriage. Although the majority of companies provide disability pay for mothers to stay home with a newborn, fathers receive nothing. Peters suggests savings plans to provide for the loss of income.

Before You Read

How would you share the care of a newborn? How would you handle the loss of income if you were to take parental leave?

Words to Know

coffers   chest for money, strongbox
compensate   pay, make up for
sequentially   one after the other, in a series
superfluous   unnecessary, not needed
transformations   changes

When our daughter was born six years ago, I briefly campaigned for 1 my husband's taking parental leave. But as most husbands would, he said, "I can't possibly. It's not done. Men don't take parental leave. A week's vacation, yes O.K.; maybe I can stretch it to two."

What he said, of course, was true. 2

Well, who cared? Who could ask for anything more than being a mother 3 anyway? Don't push your luck, I told myself. Maybe I was even glad to be left alone to moon at my beautiful baby girl. Along about the time she got her first tooth, though, I realized that forgoing paternity leave was a mistake. And by the time she lost that very same tooth, I even knew why.

Becoming a parent is surely among the most profound transforma- 4 tions a person makes. Becoming a hands-on, nurturing one is a major challenge. Particularly for men, who aren't raised to be fathers in a primary way, feeding, dressing, bathing, diapering, comforting and just being there.

Especially when the mother nurses, the father may just drift farther 5 from the enchanted bonding duo, feeling ever more superfluous, less important in his wife's eyes as well as his own now that the baby is her major concern. Rushing to the office to bolster his deflated ego, as well as fill the family's rapidly diminishing coffers, he is left behind in babyland. While his wife is becoming a parenting expert and growing ever more central to the baby, the couple can begin to grow apart. Even if she goes back to work after three months, as most women do, she's by then the manager of child care and he's clueless, calling her about every problem.

If the parents are able to move into parenthood together, riding its roller 6 coaster of fright (How did this happen to me? How do people live without sleep?) and ecstatic delight (Did you hear that? She mimicked the sound I made), both have the chance to bond deeply and develop nurturing styles.

It has to start early, though. By taking parental leave, men can set a 7 pattern for the shared parenting today's two-paycheck families cannot do without. Working mothers simply cannot do it all, at least not without the resentment that erodes a marriage.

Even if Dad is convinced that paternity leave is right for him, his mar- 8 riage, and his family, a couple still faces significant financial and scheduling hurdles.

But they don't have to take full leave at the same time. Depending on 9 their negotiations with their employers, Mom might take the first two months, then they could both work part time for another two, leaving Dad in charge for one or two days a week. They could also take leave sequentially. If she's off for three months, he may then take one or two, and believe me, he'll make up for any lost time in the primary parent department. Just knowing he'll have his turn will change the chemistry of the marriage.

Even so, the Family and Medical Leave Act only guarantees 12 weeks 10 unpaid leave to parents, though according to the Bureau of Labor Statistics, 87 percent of women employed by medium-to-large companies and 61 percent in small concerns receive disability pay to stay home with a newborn; new dads get nothing.

Saving with a minimal amount of planning and belt-tightening is cen- 11 tral to overcoming the erosion of income parental leave can cause. Taking two typical situations, here's how the numbers might work.

If she's a nurse earning $35,000, and he's a high school teacher making 12 $37,000, saving $200 a month in certificates of deposit for three years—$8,000 including interest—will be the equivalent of two months of after-tax income. That would compensate for earnings lost to parental leave for those two months. In life style terms, that saving is the difference between keeping a Honda Accord till it's worn out and leasing a Jeep Grand Cherokee every three years.

Couples earning more, a lawyer and a systems analyst, for example, 13 whose combined income is $90,000, can save $600 a month for two years, giving them $15,000, or three months of after-tax income. That might mean the difference between two five-star vacations and two weeks at a nearby lake.

Children are a big expense, and having enough time with them is an 14 ever bigger, but essential, one. Strategic planning by parents is called for, including cutting back on nonessentials like the dream house, the mini-van, and the designer nursery.

Making time for Mom and Dad to fall in love with a baby comes at a 15 cost. But being parents can be far more exciting than a trip to Paris, and it can strengthen a marriage. Particularly if she and he do it together.

Questions About the Reading

1. What reason did Peters's husband give for not taking parental leave?
2. Why is it important for the parents to "move into parenthood together"?
3. What does the writer suggest doing to handle the loss of income during parental leave?

Thinking Critically

1. If fathers should be paid while taking parental leave, who should pay them?
2. What would be the impact on businesses and companies if they are required to pay for parental leave?
3. What would be the effect on the prices of the goods and services provided by businesses and companies if they are required to pay for parental leave?

Writing Assignments

1. Write a letter to your employer asking to take paid vacation or sick time for the birth of a child.
2. Working with classmates, learn which businesses and companies in your town provide disability or other pay for the mother and unpaid parental leave for the father of a newborn child. Create a table of your findings.

What Today's Fathers Want

James A. Levine and Todd L. Pittinsky

According to James A. Levine and Todd L. Pittinsky, a majority of Ameri-can men derive greater satisfaction from caring for their family than from a job well done at work. The writers provide statistics to support their view and to show that men suffer from the same stress and conflicts as women do over balancing work and family demands.

Before You Read

What would you do if your work required you to be out of town on one of your children's graduation day?

Words to Know

deceleration   decrease in rate
gratification   satisfaction, pleasure
integration   combination, bringing together
mañana   Spanish for "tomorrow"
physiological   bodily functions and processes
predictor   indicator
simultaneous   at the same time
variables   differences, changes

Put simply, what fathers increasingly want is the ability to both provide   1
for *and* spend time with their children. Although work is an unquestion-ably powerful source of male identity and satisfaction, family is equally strong. A 1991 Gallup poll found that a majority of American men—59 percent—derive "a greater sense of satisfaction from caring for their fam-ily than from a job well done at work." In 1992 a national survey con-ducted by the Roper Organization for *Playboy* magazine found men "evenly split about whether the main focus of their life is job (31%) or family (33%)," with the other third saying "both equally." Two years later, in 1993, a nationally representative study by University of Illinois psy-chologist Joseph Pleck concluded that men now "seek their primary emo-tional, personal, and spiritual gratification from the family setting." By 1996 a Consumer Survey Center poll of men in their thirties and forties done for Levi Strauss & Co. discovered that 84 percent of baby-boomer men say that "success" means being a good father, while 72 percent cite

having a close partnership with a spouse or significant other. Poll after poll—and I have cited only a few—turns up similar results.

Does this mean that men—especially fathers—are slackening their in- 2 terest in work and career? Absolutely not. Analysis of FWI's *1997 National Study of the Changing Workforce* indicates that men in the primary child-rearing years are eager for increased challenge and responsibility: almost 53 percent of men with children under 18 want more responsibility compared to 50 percent of men without children (or with children over eighteen).

This high level of simultaneous commitment to both work and family 3 is different from a pattern observed as recently as 1983 by Fernando Bartolome of the Harvard Business School, who found many male managers taking what he termed the *mañana* approach, continually putting off family concerns until "tomorrow." But by 1994, when a Families and Work Institute/Whirlpool Foundation survey asked a representative sample of U.S. men, "What makes you feel successful at home?" the most frequent response was good family relationships and spending time together, followed by "financial security" and "being able to afford things."

The integration of work and family is not only what more and more of 4 today's fathers want; it is also what women are looking for in their marriage partners, according to a 1993 *Parents* magazine survey of its readers. In the same year, when *Child* magazine asked its readers to rank the characteristics of a "good father," both mothers and fathers gave first place to "being involved with my children's daily life," followed closely by "being able to support my family financially."

In fact, most of the U.S. population now agrees with this double-duty 5 definition of the good father, according to the Family Research Council, a conservative Washington think tank headed by Gary Bauer, former domestic policy adviser in the Reagan White House. A survey conducted for FRC by the Roper Organization in 1993 found that 76 percent of adults said that mothers and fathers should be "equally responsible" for "infant care and feeding" or for "taking care of a child who is sick or injured." When it comes to "tucking a child in bed," the number in favor of equal care jumped to 94 percent, and "helping with homework" rated 96 percent. But when it comes to earning an income, a large percentage still expects the father to be primary breadwinner. Although the same survey found that 58 percent of adults feel responsibility should be shared equally, 39 percent said breadwinning should be the primary responsibility of the father, and 3 percent said they did not know.

What these data suggest about today's families—and about today's 6 working fathers in particular—is both profound and largely ignored. "[T]he questions about juggling home and family life are always asked as if there were only one sex on the planet," say Rosalind Barnett, research scholar at the Radcliffe Institute, and journalist Caryl Rivers. "Men, it is assumed, . . . have built-in, watertight doors that separate each part of their lives. The man at work, we believe, never sits at his desk worrying about his kids."

Not true, according to an emerging body of research, as well as to ear- 7 lier research that has not received as much attention as it deserves. Since men don't often express their emotions about parenthood (or much else) as readily as women, it's easy to assume that they don't have strong feelings on these issues. But according to a multiyear study of a random sample of three hundred dual-earner couples conducted by Barnett for the National Institutes of Mental Health, men feel just as much anxiety on the job because they are fathers as women do because they are mothers: "[G]nawing concern about the children—such as worry over their safety or their choice of friends or about the financial burden they impose—can cause either parent to suffer stress-related health problems." In fact, a man's experience as a *parent*—not as an employee—was the strongest predictor of whether he would have stress-related physical symptoms. In terms of men's mental health, the roles of worker, spouse, and parent had equal significance.

That men have such strong physical and emotional reactions when 8 concerned about their children's well-being was actually revealed about twenty years ago in a fascinating study conducted by Michael Lamb, now chief of the section on social and emotional development at the National Institutes for Child Health and Development. Mothers and fathers watched and listened to a videotape of a crying baby, followed by a videotape of a smiling and cooing baby. "While they watched," Lamb explains, "we monitored parents' blood pressure, heart rate, and galvanic skin response. We found that crying babies elicited accelerated rates on all three measures, while a comfortable baby elicited a deceleration. There was no difference in reaction between mothers and fathers. For both fathers and mothers, the changes seemed to be preparing the body for behavioral responses to the baby. Deceleration leads people to continue what they are doing, whereas acceleration is an indication of anger or the body being aroused and prepared for action—presumably the action of going to the baby to relieve the distress. The same patterns in males and females suggest that both have a basic physiological response to these important signals. We repeated this test in three or four different studies with babies of different ages—preterm babies, full-term babies, and so on. And again, the physiological responses of fathers and mothers were indistinguishable."

New research reveals that, as children age, working fathers continue 9 to have strong reactions about the care of their children. Among the biggest worries of fathers today is how their children are faring in child care while they are at work. That's not what researcher Kirby Deater-Deckard at Vanderbilt University and her colleagues expected to find when they interviewed 589 dual-income married couples in Boston, Richmond, and Atlanta. They assumed fathers would be less emotionally affected than mothers by leaving their children in day care. But when they controlled for a host of other variables that might affect paternal stress—including the children's age, sex, and ethnicity, the number of children in the family, per capita income, parents' age and education, even attitudes toward traditional gender roles in the family—they discovered that fathers feel as much, and sometimes more, anxiety about separating from their preschoolers in day care as mothers do. Furthermore, fathers who are more satisfied with their child-care arrangements feel less stressed at work, more satisfied in their role as parents, and more satisfied with their lives in general, according to FWI's *1992 National Study of the Changing Workforce*.

Stress over child care, long a major worry for the 23 percent of the mothers in the workforce who are single parents, is increasingly being shared by the 4 percent of working fathers who are single parents. Some are men like Stuart Browy of Columbia, South Carolina, who now has what he calls the "3 P.M. syndrome" under reasonable control, thanks to support from his employer, National Cash Register. "My eleven- and thirteen-year-old sons call me at my office just to let me know they are safe." But others, like Alan Smith, a single father in the rural town of Brimfield, Massachusetts, struggle with their employers. Smith's day job with the U.S. Postal Service was eliminated, and he was told he had to work nights. "I told them I could not work nights because I had a ten-year-old son and I am a single parent. I cannot afford child care on one income, plus I would not be able to be a parent for my son. Being with my son two days a week is not a good way to be a parent. They said they don't care. The topper is, they hired temps to do my day job. I just don't know where to turn."

Whether in single- or dual-parent families, one of the common denominators among working fathers is feeling torn by two emotions: guilt for not spending more time with their children and worry about being able to make a living. Jack Simonetti, professor of management at the University of Toledo, and his colleagues surveyed 330 middle-class baby-boomer parents in 1993. Contrary to prevailing opinion, the study revealed that working mothers do not have a monopoly on guilt: 47 percent of fathers said they do not spend enough "quality time" with their children. And when they are unable to spend more time with their families, 78 percent of the men say they feel guilty "often/always" or "sometimes," compared to 70 percent of the women, who expressed more confidence in the time they spent with their children. It's a double bind, expressed aptly by Chris Celentino, a bankruptcy attorney and partner in a San Diego, California, law firm. "You work longer hours because of the fear that you're not providing enough. Then there's the guilt that you're not spending enough time with your family. It goes around and around. You work harder for stability, and it gives you less stability than you think."

"There's always conflict," says Stephen Roache, a father of two sons, 12
ages eight and ten, who works as director of finance for the Harlem School of the Arts. "I often feel guilty because I probably missed a Boy Scout meeting or whatever. My older son is in Boy Scouts, softball, and basketball. My younger son is in piano and Jack and Jill, a group for African-American boys. On a typical day I'm up at 6:30 A.M., shower, make breakfast, fix lunches, and get them out to the bus stop. My wife presses their clothes before she leaves for work. I'm home by about 8 P.M. At the end of the day I get a half an hour with them before they go to bed. On weekends I take one of my sons to piano and Cub Scouts. I just need a day to do what I want, to read a book, read the *Times* cover to cover. I love what I do, but if I'm going to make any more money it will be at the same pace. There's no getting around that in this day and age."

Questions About the Reading

1. What was the commitment of men to work and family in 1983? How did it differ from their commitment in 1994?
2. What are women looking for in their marriage partners, according to a *Parents* magazine survey? How does the women's view differ from that of men?
3. According to a 1993 survey by the Roper Organization, who should be responsible for child care and homework: the father or the mother? Who should be the primary breadwinner?
4. What two emotions are common among working fathers concerning their children?

Thinking Critically

1. How would you suggest that parents divide their working and child care responsibilities so that they feel less stress?
2. How would you suggest resolving a conflict between a required out-of-town trip for work and your child's graduation from school?

Writing Assignments

1. Write a letter to your employer explaining your conflict between an out-of-town business trip and your child's graduation. Suggest a solution.
2. In your journal, list the responsibilities of a husband and a wife in maintaining a household and family (cooking, cleaning, shopping, child care) and the time each task should take.
3. Create a table from your journal list of household maintenance tasks.

Still Seeking the Perfect Balance

Elizabeth McGuire

Elizabeth McGuire was a graduate student at Johns Hopkins School of Advanced International Studies when she wrote this article for the New York Times.

Before You Read

How will you balance the demands of education, work, and marriage?

Words to Know

embroiled   involved emotionally

hiatus   break, pause

progressive   forward-looking

stamina   endurance

As a first-year law student, my future husband, Kris, walked into the 1
school's career counseling office to ask about strategies for combining a successful career with a happy family life. The surprised (female) counselors gave him compliments for his progressive attitude—but not a single word of practical advice.

We weren't even engaged at the time, but we already were embroiled 2
in a series of deep discussions—negotiations, really—about our plans for both family and careers.

In the four years since then, I have talked to women of all ages about 3
balancing work and family life. What has surprised me the most is the difference in outlook between women my age, 27, and women just 10 years older.

Women in their late 30s and older felt they had few choices in a male 4
work culture that pretended family obligations didn't exist. Some of them waited to have children until their late 30s and early 40s, when they had built a solid foundation for their careers and could afford a hiatus. Others had children at a younger age, but hired full-time nannies or day-care providers to take care of them. Still others simply left their jobs for good once their children were born.

But most women I know who are in their 20s are dissatisfied with these 5
alternatives. Concerned about infertility, many of us want to have chil-

dren while we're young. And though many of the dual-career couples I know who have nannies are wonderful parents and have successful careers, their relationships with each other seem to have suffered.

While others debate whether day care is harmful to children, we are 6 more worried about avoiding the frenetic pace these families seem to keep. At the same time, many of us are ambitious and do not want to become stay-at-home moms just to attain a measure of peace.

So many young women I know are trying to find new options. That 7 means making career decisions to balance work and family years before we intend to have children.

Many of my friends are getting graduate degrees not just to further 8 their careers, but also to give them flexibility when they have children. Others are choosing family-friendly employers or staying at jobs in the hopes that they will be repaid with more flexibility. Some friends are even starting their own businesses.

Yet perhaps the greatest generational change has occurred in our mar- 9 riages. More and more of us seek husbands who are willing to sacrifice some ambition to spend time with their children and are happy to share the role of breadwinner with their wives.

For my husband and me, equality has meant taking turns in concen- 10 trating on our careers. While he was in law school, I took care of most of the housework and stayed in a low-key job to support his efforts. But now that I'm pursuing master's degrees in business administration and international affairs, he's returning the favor. He took a job in a small firm that respects its lawyers' personal lives, and he does almost all the work around the house. Men in older generations may have helped out, but they still didn't clean the bathroom. And most of them didn't factor in their families when they mapped out their careers.

Kris and I are pleased with our success so far, but the balance may not 11 be so easy to maintain in the future. We probably will encounter some of the same obstacles that past generations did—the lack of part-time jobs and flexible work hours, and corporate cultures that frown on people taking leaves of absence for child-rearing.

If Gen-X'ers don't succeed in forcing a shift in the very concept of a 12 "career," the balance between work and family we desire will remain out of our reach. Instead of the traditional corporate ladder, which emphasizes stamina, we must seek a model of career progress that resembles mountain climbing, which requires flexibility, lateral moves, and lengthy rests at base camp.

Many people may think we are nearing the end of the workplace revo- 13 lution. In reality, we are only just beginning.

Questions About the Reading

1. What does the writer say is the attitude of women in their thirties and older about family obligations and having children?
2. How does the attitude of women in their twenties toward family obligations and children differ from that of women in their thirties and older?
3. According to the writer, why are many women getting graduate degrees?
4. What is the model the writer suggests for career progress?

Thinking Critically

1. How do you plan to balance your education, work, and family responsibilities?
2. What should be the responsibilities of each family member?

Writing Assignments

1. In your journal, list five factors that are important to you in choosing a career.
2. Write an essay in which you explain how the five factors might affect your personal or family life.

4

Ethics

MAKING A DECISION can be difficult, especially if the decision involves a choice that is to the benefit of your workplace but is in conflict with your personal ethics. In "What Is Ethics Anyway?" O. C. Farrell and Gareth Gardiner define ethics and give examples of possible workplace and personal ethics conflicts. Humorist Calvin Trillin finds a twenty-dollar bill in the street and tells us, in "The Twenty-Dollar Bill," of his reluctance to turn it in to the police.

Michael Korda, in "Defining Success," and Ellen Goodman, in "It's Failure, Not Success," disagree over the ethics and morality needed for a person to get ahead or succeed in their careers. In "Unethical Workers and Illegal Acts," the results of a survey reveal that nearly half of the 1,324 worker respondents admitted to committing illegal acts, ranging from theft to violating environmental laws, at work. John Davidson, in "The Business of Ethics," tells us that a growing number of companies have established ethics programs to address the problem of illegal employee actions.

Memorandums

In this chapter you will be asked to write a memorandum, or memo. The purpose of a memo is to provide the recipient with information quickly and in a clear, focused format. An example of a memo to a classmate in your collaborative writing group follows. Notice the headings used in the memo: date, to, from, subject.

[Date]

To: [Name of person to whom you are writing]

From: [Your name] [Your handwritten initials]

Subject: Collaborative Group Meeting

Our collaborative writing group will meet in the Student Center Conference Room on October 6 at 9:00 A.M.

Please bring your completed assignment with you. We will expect to
complete the first draft of our report at this meeting.

Notice that you should add your initials after your name before sending
the memo.

   Now suppose that you want to write a report about the bids you have
received for towel bindings and send it to the vice president of manufacturing of your company, ABC Towel Company. Your company may have
memo letterhead or special memo paper, which you should use. Your
memo might look like the following example:

ABC TOWEL COMPANY

INTEROFFICE MEMORANDUM

December 15, 2000

To: Clyde Sheridan

           Vice President, Manufacturing

From: John Wilson   *JW*

           Purchasing Manufacturing

Subject: Binding Bids

I have received the following bids for the bindings you requested:

Fletcher Binding

5,000 yds	$\frac{1}{2}$ inch	White cotton	.02 per yd.
3,000 yds	1 inch	White 60/40 cotton/polyester	.03 per yd.
2,000 yds	1 inch	Green cotton	.03 per yd.
2,000 yds	$\frac{1}{2}$ inch	Green 60/40 cotton/polyester	.04 per yd.

W. B. Martin Company

5,000 yds	½ inch	White cotton	.01 per yd.
3,000 yds	1 inch	White 60/40 cotton/polyester	.02 per yd.
2,000 yds	1 inch	Green cotton	.04 per yd.
2,000 yds	½ inch	Green 60/40 cotton/polyester	.05 per yd.

Jackson Williard Company

5,000 yds	½ inch	White cotton	.03 per yd.
3,000 yds	1 inch	White 60/40 cotton/polyester	.04 per yd.
2,000 yds	1 inch	Green cotton	.02 per yd.
2,000 yds	½ inch	Green 60/40 cotton/polyester	.03 per yd.

Jackson Williard Company came in at .01 per yd. more than Fletcher and .02 more than Martin on the white bindings, but .01 under Fletcher and .02 under Martin on the green bindings. I suggest we order the white bindings from Fletcher and the green bindings from Jackson Williard.

With your approval, I will proceed with the order as suggested above.

Notice that the writer has provided the specific information that the recipient of the memo needs to make a decision and has been brief and clear.

What Is Ethics Anyway?

O. C. Farrell and Gareth Gardiner

In this excerpt from their book, In Pursuit of Ethics, *O. C. Farrell and Gareth Gardiner define ethics and discuss the problem of making ethical decisions in the workplace.*

Before You Read

How would you handle a workplace decision that you think is unethical?

Words to Know

criteria standards, rules, factors
deceptive misleading
inalienable cannot be taken away, cannot be transferred
infringe break, ignore, disregard
surreptitiously secretly, furtively

The average American has a pretty good common-sense understand- 1
ing of what an *ethical* act or decision is: It is something judged as proper or acceptable based on some standard of right and wrong. Although people often have different morals and standards of right and wrong, many are shared by most members of our society. Note that we cannot tell you what is right or wrong for you in a specific situation. At a minimum, of course, an activity should be legal; most authorities on ethics agree that the law generally defines the minimum level of conduct that is acceptable in a given situation.

We agree with this common understanding of the term, but we would 2
also like to propose two additional criteria that we believe are important in helping people make ethical decisions in the workplace. First, some people believe that an ethical act is one that leads to the greatest benefit for the most people (utilitarianism), or one that does not infringe on the basic inalienable human rights—such as life, freedom of speech and privacy, due process—recognized by our society (ethical formalism). Second, an ethical act is one that increases the self-esteem and mental health of the person engaging in that act, particularly in the long run, but it may also expose the person to a great deal of short-term stress.

The first criterion may be recognized as a simple restatement of the 3
two most common philosophies for dealing with ethical decisions. The

92

second criterion, having to do with maintaining one's self-esteem or self-respect, is another old idea, but one to which modern psychologists and philosophers have returned. These contemporary thinkers say that maintaining one's self-respect is important, but this does not mean for a moment that it is easy, or even desirable, in every situation where an ethical choice may have to be made.

This thought leads to another statement about ethics and ethical choices: 4 Making ethical choices is often a difficult and complex process for anyone, and it is not always obvious or even easy to identify what is the right or "correct" choice. Any choice in a given situation often involves some degree of conflict or pain. . . .

One reason that making ethical choices in business is so often trouble- 5 some is that business ethics is not simply an extension of an individual's personal ethics. Just being a good person and, in your own view, having high ethical standards may not be enough to handle the tough choices that frequently arise in the workplace. People with limited business experience often must make decisions about complex issues such as product quality, advertising, pricing, hiring practices, and pollution control. The moral standards they learned from their families and in church and school may not be easily translated to the business world. For example, is a particular advertisement deceptive? Should a gift to a customer be considered a bribe, or is it a "special promotional incentive"? What about surreptitiously discharging a little toxic waste into the local creek rather than spending the money to dispose of it properly, thereby avoiding the need to raise prices charged to customers? In other words, our experiences at home, church, school, and in the community are often quite different from those we face at work, and thus may leave us woefully unprepared when confronted with tough choices in the workplace.

Questions About the Reading

1. What do the writers say is the minimum standard for an ethical act or decision?
2. What are the two criteria the writers offer for making ethical decisions in the workplace?
3. Which of the two criteria is favored by modern psychologists and philosophers?
4. Why is it troublesome to make ethical choices in business?

Thinking Critically

1. What would you do if the company you work for discharged toxic waste into a creek or river in your city to avoid having to raise the cost of the company's product?
2. What would you do if the advertising for your company's product made inaccurate claims?

Writing Assignments

1. Write a memo to your supervisor asking for a meeting to discuss the advertising for your company's product.
2. You find out that your company's product contains a chemical that could be harmful and is not listed on its label. Working with classmates, find out what laws cover product-labeling and write a memo, including an informal report, to the head of your company's research department advising her of the problem.

The Twenty-Dollar Bill

Calvin Trillin

Calvin Trillin writes for The New Yorker, Time, *and* The Nation *magazines and is the author of nineteen books. In this chapter from his book* Family Man, *he demonstrates honesty, although with some reluctance, when he finds a twenty-dollar bill and turns it over to the police.*

Before You Read

What would you do if you found a wallet containing money and credit cards?

Words to Know

Bellevue   psychiatric hospital in New York City
cynicism   scorn, doubt

... Although I rather doubt that many parents are able to alter their normal behavior in the long run by remembering that they're setting an example for their children, there are obviously examples of short-term alterations—the time, for instance, when I found a twenty-dollar bill on Hudson Street. 1

Quite late one evening, when the girls were still small, Alice and I were walking toward our house, in Greenwich Village, when I spotted a twenty-dollar bill on the sidewalk. As I picked it up, Alice said, "You'll have to turn it in." I must have given her a puzzled look, because she added, "Some poor person could have dropped it." The next morning, she reminded me that I was going to go over to the Sixth Precinct to turn in the twenty. 2

"It's not that I believe in keeping property that is not my own," I said. "As you know, I was strictly raised about such matters. Of course, that was in Kansas City, in a different era. In New York these days, I think it's fair to say, there's a certain amount of cynicism abroad—big city, different times, and all that. What I'm afraid of, frankly, is that I'll walk into the Sixth Precinct, announce that I want to turn in twenty dollars in cash that I found on Hudson Street late at night, and get myself hauled off to Bellevue as a loony. I've heard they can keep you there twenty-four hours for observation, no matter what." 3

"I've already told the girls that you're going over there to turn it in," 4
Alice said. She could have just as easily said, "I've been officially informed

by a representative of the Lord that if you don't turn in the twenty-dollar
bill a bolt of lightning will fry you to a crisp."

"I'm off," I said, reaching for my coat.   5

The sergeant at the Sixth Precinct did not have me hauled off to Bellevue. 6
He just said something like "Let me get this straight: you found this
twenty-dollar bill last night and you want to turn it in for somebody to
claim?"

"That's right, Sergeant," I said. I had decided not to trouble him with   7
the part about the poor person.

He exchanged glances with a patrolman who was sitting nearby. Then   8
he reached for a form, and began to fill it out. A sergeant who worked in
the Sixth Precinct, which is responsible for the Village, was obviously
someone who'd been exposed to a broad range of human behavior. For
all I knew, there could be a man on Perry Street who regularly turned in
his own fifties, just as a sort of hobby. A few months later, to my amaze-
ment, I got a notice from police headquarters downtown that, the twenty
having gone unclaimed, I could come down and pick it up. I did. I told
the girls.

Questions About the Reading

1. Why did Trillin's wife think he should turn in the twenty-dollar bill?
2. Why was he reluctant to turn the bill in to the police?
3. What did his wife say that convinced Trillin he had to turn the bill in?
4. What happened after he turned in the bill that amazed Trillin?

Thinking Critically

1. If you found a wallet containing money and credit cards, what would
   you do and how would you do it?
2. If someone called you and said that they had found your lost wallet
   containing money and credit cards, what would you do?
3. What do you think would happen if you found a twenty-dollar bill
   and turned it in to the police in your town?

Writing Assignments

1. Write a letter to the person whose wallet you have found.
2. Write a letter to the person who found your wallet.

Defining Success

Michael Korda

Michael Korda has written several books with the intention of helping people get the most out of their work and their lives. The titles of his books tell you exactly what he has in mind for you—Power! and Success! But before he can tell you (as the subtitle of his first book puts it) "how to get it, how to use it," he wants to be sure you understand what it is. In the first chapter of Success! he presents this controversial definition.

Before You Read

What is your personal definition of *success*?

Words to Know

conglomerate   a business corporation made up of many different companies

degenerate   to decrease in quality or size

grandiose   large, great

relative   determined in relation to something else

superseded   taken over, replaced

unethical   lacking in honesty or principles

———————

Others may ask how you define success. This is more difficult. Success is   1
relative; not everybody wants to put together a four-billion-dollar conglomerate, or become President of the United States, or win the Nobel Peace
Prize. It is usually a mistake to begin with such grandiose ambitions, which
tend to degenerate into lazy daydreams. The best way to succeed is to
begin with a reasonably realistic goal and attain it, rather than aiming at
something so far beyond your reach that you are bound to fail. It's also
important to make a habit of succeeding, and the easiest way to start is to
succeed at something, however small, every day, gradually increasing the
level of your ambitions and achievements like a runner in training, who
begins with short distances and works up to Olympic levels.

Try to think of success as a journey, an adventure, not a specific desti-   2
nation. Your goals may change during the course of that journey, and
your original ambitions may be superseded by different, larger ones. Success will certainly bring you the material things you want, and a good,
healthy appetite for the comforts and luxuries of life is an excellent road

to success, but basically you'll know you have reached your goal when you have gone that one step further, in wealth, fame, or achievement, than you ever dreamed was possible.

How you become a success is, of course, your business. Morality has   3 very little to do with success. I do not personally think it is necessary to be dishonest, brutal, or unethical in order to succeed, but a great many dishonest, brutal, or unethical people in fact do succeed. You'd better be prepared for the fact that success is seldom won without some tough in-fighting along the way. A lot depends on your profession, of course. There is a great deal of difference between setting out to become a success in a Mafia family and trying to become vice president of a bank, but the dif-ferences simply consist of contrasting social customs and of what is the appropriate way to get ahead in a given profession or business. Whether you're hoping to take over a numbers game or an executive desk, you have to make the right moves for your circumstances. In the former ex-ample, you might have to kill someone; in the latter, you might only have to find ways of making your rivals look foolish or inefficient. In either case, you have to accept the rules of the game and play to win, or find some other game. This is a book about success, after all, not morality. The field you go into is your choice, but whatever it is, you're better off at the top of it than at the bottom.

Questions About the Reading

1. What does the writer say is the best way to succeed?
2. What does the writer mean when he says, "Try to think of success as a journey, an adventure, not a specific destination"? Does this sentence in any way contradict what he says is the best way to succeed?
3. What does Korda mean by his statement "Morality has very little to do with success"?
4. What does Korda suggest you do if you have to violate your moral standards to achieve success in your field?

Thinking Critically

1. What do you think you need to do to get ahead in your occupation? How would you go about doing it?
2. What personal qualities do you think are the most important in suc-ceeding in the occupation you are considering?

Writing Assignments

1. In your journal, assess your personal qualities. Use a scale of 1–5, with 5 being "outstanding" or "excellent."
2. Write an essay explaining what you think you need to achieve to be successful in life.

It's Failure, Not Success

Ellen Goodman

Not everyone agrees with Michael Korda's get-what-you-can mentality (see pp. 97–99). Ellen Goodman found herself getting more and more disturbed as she read Korda's words to live by. She was certain there must be more to the truly successful life. So she wrote her own definition of success and applied another term, failure, to the self-serving life Korda described. Do you agree with Korda or with Goodman?

Before You Read

In what ways could success be accompanied by failure?

Words to Know

ambivalence   simultaneously having different feelings or attitudes

bigot   an intolerant or prejudiced person

edits   cuts out, does away with

excised   removed

Fanny Farmer   author of a well-known cookbook

finesses   glosses over

intent   determined

judgmental   having an opinion about something, criticizing it

machete-ing   using a machete or heavy knife

Machiavellian   having political principles that are based on craftiness and doing anything necessary to get ahead

napalm   a firm jelly used in flame throwers and incendiary bombs

placebo   a substance given as medication but does not contain actual medication

---

I knew a man who went into therapy about three years ago because, as 1 he put it, he couldn't live with himself any longer. I didn't blame him. The guy was a bigot, a tyrant, and a creep.

In any case, I ran into him again after he'd finished therapy. He was 2 still a bigot, a tyrant, and a creep, *but* . . . he had learned to live with himself.

Now, I suppose this was an accomplishment of sorts. I mean, nobody 3 else could live with him. But it seems to me that there are an awful lot of

100

people running around and writing around these days encouraging us to feel good about what we should feel terrible about, and to accept in ourselves what we should change.

The only thing they seem to disapprove of is disapproval. The only 4 judgment they make is against being judgmental, and they assure us that we have nothing to feel guilty about except guilt itself. It seems to me that they are all intent on proving that I'm OK and You're OK, when in fact, I may be perfectly dreadful and you may be unforgivably dreary, and it may be–gasp!–*wrong.*

What brings on my sudden attack of judgmentitis is success, or rather, 5 *Success!*–the latest in a series of exclamation-point books all concerned with How to Make it.

In this one, Michael Korda is writing a recipe book for success. Like 6 the other authors, he leapfrogs right over the "Shoulds" and into the "Hows." He eliminates value judgments and edits out moral questions as if he were Fanny Farmer and the subject was the making of a blueberry pie.

It's not that I have any reason to doubt Mr. Korda's advice on the way 7 to achieve success. It may very well be that successful men wear handkerchiefs stuffed neatly in their breast pockets, and that successful single women should carry suitcases to the office on Fridays whether or not they are going away for the weekend.

He may be realistic when he says that "successful people generally 8 have very low expectations of others." And he may be only slightly cynical when he writes: "One of the best ways to ensure success is to develop expensive tastes or marry someone who has them."

And he may be helpful with his handy hints on how to sit next to some- 9 one you are about to overpower.

But he simply finesses the issues of right and wrong—silly words, em- 10 barrassing words that have been excised like warts from the shiny surface of the new how-to books. To Korda, guilt is not a prod, but an enemy that he slays on page four. Right off the bat, he tells the would-be successful reader that:

- It's OK to be greedy.
- It's OK to look out for Number One.
- It's OK to be Machiavellian (if you can get away with it).
- It's OK to recognize that honesty is not always the best policy (provided you don't go around saying so).
- And it's always OK to be rich.

Well, in fact, it's not OK. It's not OK to be greedy, Machiavellian, dis- 11 honest. It's not always OK to be rich. There is a qualitative difference between succeeding by making napalm or by making penicillin. There is a difference between climbing the ladder of success, and machete-ing a path to the top.

Only someone with the moral perspective of a mushroom could as- 12 sure us that this was all OK. It seems to me that most Americans harbor ambivalence toward success, not for neurotic reasons, but out of a realistic perception of what it demands.

Success is expensive in terms of time and energy and altered behav- 13 ior—the sort of behavior he describes in the grossest of terms: "If you can undermine your boss and replace him, fine, do so, but never express anything but respect and loyalty for him while you're doing it."

This author—whose *Power!* topped the best-seller list last year—is in- 14 tent on helping rid us of that ambivalence which is a signal from our conscience. He is like the other "Win!" "Me First!" writers, who try to make us comfortable when we should be uncomfortable.

They are all Doctor Feelgoods, offering us placebo prescriptions in- 15 stead of strong medicine. They give us a way to live with ourselves, perhaps, but not a way to live with each other. They teach us a whole lot more about "Failure!" than about success.

Questions About the Reading

1. What does the writer mean when she says, "[H]e leapfrogs right over the 'Shoulds' and into the 'Hows'"?
2. What is the "qualitative difference between succeeding by making napalm or by making penicillin"?
3. What is the "moral perspective of a mushroom"? Does Korda have such a perspective, in your opinion?
4. What does success demand that makes Americans ambivalent about it? What is it about Korda's brand of success that should make us uncomfortable?

Thinking Critically

1. Which of the five competencies do you think may be most important in the occupation you are considering? How do you think that competency would contribute to your succeeding in your chosen occupation?
2. How do you think the foundation skills will be used in the occupation you are considering?

Writing Assignments

1. Working with classmates, write an essay identifying three persons you consider successful and explain why you consider them successful.
2. Working with classmates, write an informal report identifying the skills and competencies required for success in professional sports.

Unethical Workers and Illegal Acts

Society *Magazine*

Workers, managers, and executives admit to committing unethical acts at their workplace due to pressure, and they admit that the situation is getting worse. Even though most employee theft goes unreported, according to the writer, it costs companies an estimated $120 billion a year.

Before You Read

What do you think companies can do to reduce or eliminate unethical acts by their employees?

Words to Know

attributed   assigned, credited
fraudulent   illegal, deceitful
oxymoron   contradictory, foolish statement
phenomenal   huge, unusual

Nearly half, 48 percent, of U.S. workers admit to unethical or illegal acts 1
during 1996. Those include one or more from a list of 25 actions, including cheating on an expense account, discriminating against coworkers, paying or accepting kickbacks, secretly forging signatures, trading sex for sales, and looking the other way when environmental laws are violated.

The survey of 1,324 randomly selected workers, managers, and execu- 2
tives in multiple industries was sponsored by the Ethics Officer Association and the American Society of Chartered Life Underwriters & Chartered Financial Consultants. The 236-page report is especially sobering because workers were asked only to list violations that they attributed to "pressure" due to such things as long hours, sales quotas, job insecurity, balancing work and family, and personal debt. It didn't ask about unethical or illegal action for other reasons such as greed, revenge, and blind ambition. The survey's margin of error is plus or minus 3 percentage points.

Also sobering is that workers say it's getting worse. Fifty-seven per- 3
cent say they feel more pressure to be unethical than five years ago and 40 percent say it's gotten worse over the last year.

Lapses Vary

Many workers might consider some of the 25 ethical violations far less 4
serious, such as calling in sick when they're feeling well. But that's really

theft of time, and the problem is "just phenomenal," says Cindy Franklin, president of Background Bureau, a company in the booming business of checking the backgrounds of job applicants.

Constant ethical violations have made workers so callous that decep- 5 tion passes for good salesmanship, Franklin says. "If someone can talk me into buying an $8,000 copier rather than one that sells for $4,200, they're going to get a pat on the back. I see that as unethical if all I need is the $4,200 model."

But unethical and illegal action by employees is taking a heavy toll. 6 Most employee theft goes unreported, but employee-screening company Guards-mark estimates it at $120 billion a year. Retail stores lose more to employee theft than to shoplifting, according to a University of Florida survey. Entry-level restaurant and fast food employees confidentially admit to stealing an average $239 a year in cash and merchandise, according to a separate survey by McGraw-Hill/London House.

Another survey of 2,500 cases of employee fraud by the Association of 7 Certified Fraud Examiners says small businesses suffered a median loss of $120,000 per occurrence. A survey by CCH shows that the more sick leave companies give employees, the more days they call in sick. The federal government successfully sues for more than $100 million a year, mostly from defense contractors and doctors and hospitals that overbill. That's four times the rate it recovered 10 years ago, says Peter Chatfield, a partner at the law firm Phillips & Cohen, which has eight full-time lawyers working on fraudulent billing against the government.

Although the survey blames ethics violations on pressure, workers in 8 marketing/advertising reported themselves to be under the least pressure to be unethical, yet committed more unethical acts than any other industry except that of computers and software.

Most ethics experts agree that job pressure is the leading cause of un- 9 ethical behavior by workers. And if anyone doubts pressure exists: 2.4 percent of all workers and 3.2 percent of senior executives have considered suicide over the past year due to pressure, the survey found. Among senior executives who happened to fill out the questionnaire during a time of high stress, 5.4 percent said they were contemplating suicide.

Workers in manufacturing and health care reported the most pressure 10 to act unethically or illegally. But they do not act on it nearly as often as computer/software workers.

Those high-tech employees say they are more than twice as likely as 11 the average worker to put inappropriate pressure on others, withhold important information, discriminate against coworkers, engage in copyright/software infringement, forge someone's name, and misuse or steal company property.

The survey was taken during good economic times. Pressure, and re- 12 sulting ethics violations, would likely turn worse in an economic slump.

Yet there are nuggets of hope in the ethics survey. In a "startling shift 13 in public opinion," only 15 percent of U.S. workers surveyed believe poor ethics is an inevitable byproduct of business, says Ed Petry, executive director of the Ethics Officer Association. "In the late 1970s and 1980s, business ethics was an oxymoron, a contradiction in terms."

The need to meet said budget or profit goals ranked sixth among 23 14 factors that workers said could trigger them to act unethically or illegally. Other top factors include balancing work and family, poor leadership, work hours and work load, and little recognition for achievements.

Other survey findings: 15

- Most workers feel some pressure to act unethically or illegally on the job (56 percent), but far fewer (17 percent) feel a high level of pressure to do so. Forty-eight percent say they actually made at least one unethical or illegal action in the past year.
- Mid-level managers most often reported a high level of pressure to act unethically or illegally (20 percent). Employees of large companies cited such pressure more than those at small businesses (21 percent vs. 14 percent)
- High levels of pressure were reported more often by those with a high school diploma or less (21 percent) vs. college graduates (13 percent).
- Men (74 percent) and women (78 percent) say they feel their families have been neglected to some extent because of workplace pressure. Women (34 percent) more than men (24 percent) say balancing work and family causes significant pressure.
- Workers say the best ways to curb ethical violations are better communication and more open dialogue (73 percent), and serious commitment by management to address the issue (71 percent).
- The most common ethical (16.1 percent) violation is cutting corners on quality control. Nearly 1 in 10 say they lied to customers and 1 in 20 lied to superiors. One out of every 40 workers say that, due to pressure, they had an affair with a business associate or contact.

Questions About the Reading

1. According to the survey, what were the illegal actions that the workers admitted doing?

2. According to the survey cited in paragraph 2, what were the reasons that workers gave for committing illegal acts?
3. What is the opinion of the public regarding business ethics according to the 1996 survey? How has public opinion changed since the 1970s and 1980s?
4. Which group feels the highest level of pressure to commit illegal acts: workers with a high school diploma or less, or college graduates?

Thinking Critically

1. What would you do if your employer wanted you to include information in an advertisement for your company's product that you knew was inaccurate?
2. What would you do if a coworker asked you to take one of your tools home and it was against company policy for tools to be taken from the workplace?

Writing Assignments

1. Write a memo to your employer in which you point out that information she wants included in an advertisement is inaccurate and refuse to include the information.
2. Develop a table using at least three of the statistics listed under "Other survey findings."

The Business of Ethics

John Davidson

In response to the 1980s moral climate of the corporate world, more and more companies have established ethics programs for their employees. They also sponsor ethics training in public schools. John Davidson discusses these trends in the following selection.

Before You Read

Do you think it is dishonest for a job applicant to omit information about a juvenile arrest on an employment application?

Words to Know

amoral   lacking morality or values
clarification   improved understanding
dilemmas   puzzles, arguments
perceive   think, believe
squalor   filth, foulness

For those of us who experienced the moral climate of the corporate world 1
in the '80s, it's a shock to discover that ethics has become an industry—a
billion-dollar growth industry. Ten years ago, ethics programs in companies were rare; the business world was exultantly Darwinian, a dog-
eat-dog, corporation-devour-corporation kind of place. The marketplace
was by definition amoral, but we celebrated it nonetheless.

Today, 45 percent of companies with 500 or more employees have eth- 2
ics programs. The Ethics Officer Association, founded in 1991, has more
than 400 members, many employed by Fortune 500 companies, and there
are 75 to 100 centers for business ethics scattered around the country. Not
only are corporations concerned with internal conduct, they're also sponsoring ethics training in public schools. In the ultimate case of
privatization, some companies contend that they are taking over the role
of government in teaching values and citizenship.

The relationship between today's ethics boom and the moral squalor 3
of the "greed is good" '80s is not coincidental. It began in 1986, when the
Reagan administration appointed a congressional commission to investigate the scandal-plagued defense industry. The commission threatened
the industry with federal policing if it didn't clean up its act. Leading
defense companies responded by joining together to pass the Defense

Industry Initiative (DII), which included a recommendation that companies establish ethics training. In 1991, when Congress revised the Federal Sentencing Guidelines for Organizations to include provisions that would make penalties harsher and more consistent for white-collar crimes, the DII recommendations were written into the revisions. According to the guidelines, penalties could be mitigated for corporations that had ethics programs; the fines for miscreant companies without them could be as much as four times higher.

Winning Employees Over

The bottom-line implications of failing to encourage ethical behavior are   4
all too obvious—Texaco's loss in a race-discrimination suit with a $154 million judgment against the company, the Archer Daniels Midland Co.'s $100 million fine for price fixing, Mercury Finance's $2.2 billion drop in stock values due to overstating profits. But ethics can also be the glue that holds a corporation together, says Carol Marshall, vice president of ethics and business conduct at Lockheed Martin Corp. "In 1995, the Lockheed Martin merger brought together 16 corporate cultures," Marshall explains. "We needed a process that would unite these diverse cultures, and talking about values and principles was a way to do it. After the merger, the board of directors adopted six core values as our code of conduct. We want people to bring their personal values to work and not park them at the door."

Lockheed Martin initiated what Marshall refers to as "top-down cas-   5
cade training." The chairman of the board trains the staffers who report directly to him. They in turn train their staff. Eventually, all 200,000 employees hear the same core message delivered at annual training sessions. Lockheed Martin also created The Ethics Challenge, a board game based on the "Dilbert" comic strip in which players must deal with ethical dilemmas, and set up a toll-free helpline for employees. "When we started the helpline in 1995, one-third of the calls were anonymous," says Marshall, "but the number has been decreasing and is down by 25 percent. This is an important statistic. It means that people trust the process. They are no longer willing to subvert their personal values to the bottom line."

Diversity in the workplace has played a prominent role in the ethics   6
industry. "We're now living in a multicultural world, and we can't assume that everyone thinks the same way," says Michael Daigneault, president of the Ethics Resource Center in Washington, D.C. "The influx of women, for example, fostered a genuine dialogue about ethics and gender issues. Because of women, we've had to stop and think about the relationship between individuals and what we expect of each other."

But for many companies, these internal programs come too late. "Com- 7
panies no longer know who they've got working for them," says Michael
Josephson, founder of the Josephson Institute of Ethics in Marina del Rey,
California. "In one survey, 25 to 40 percent of high school students say
they would lie on a résumé; 39 percent say they've stolen something in
the last year; two-thirds say they've cheated on an exam." How does this
show up in the workplace? "Twenty percent of the workers in one survey
said they had lied to their employer about something important in the
last year," Josephson says. "Sixty percent said they had a low level of
confidence in the integrity of their corporation's internal reports, and 33
percent believed there was a 'kill the messenger syndrome' that forced
them to lie and cover up. Corporations have made tremendous investments in literacy because they need workers who can read. Now they're
investing in moral literacy because they also need an honest work force."

Taking the Message Public

For that reason, companies are moving more forcefully into the commu- 8
nity. "Through their programs, corporations are taking on a new leadership role in society," says Daigneault. "They are an important influence
in people's lives. They're positively reinforcing people, saying that it's
okay to talk about values and ethical principles. People used to look to
the government to teach values. Companies have begun to take over that
role.

"Take the public schools," Daigneault continues. "There was a time 9
when most people believed the school system's job was to educate children and to create good citizens. Then, in the 1950s and '60s, schools
adopted a philosophy of 'values clarification.' Instead of telling students
what to think, teachers would lead them through the process of examining values. When the big problems were gum chewing and talking in
class, values clarification worked fine. These days, the big problems are
rape, weapons, and drugs, and values clarification isn't as useful."

The current antidote is "character education," which teaches the basic 10
values—honesty, respect for others—that society expects of its members.
Bell Atlantic Corp., in conjunction with the Ethics Resource Center, has
developed a curriculum package for character education that it is making available to school administrators nationwide. Jacquelyn B. Gates,
Bell Atlantic's ethics VP, says the company got interested in public education because employees were calling its ethics hotline with concerns
about their children's schools. "If people perceive that corporations have
the responsibility to intervene," says Daigneault, "it's because corporations have the power."

With major corporations pushing values, one has to wonder what the 11 larger effect on society might be. Are we headed toward, if not the Age of Aquarius, a more moral climate?

"There are hopeful signs," says Michael Josephson, "but you can't point 12 to any social change. Ethics might be just another issue du jour, like total quality management, risk taking, and thinking outside the box. Phases and fads go through the corporate world. We trained 2,000 IRS employees, yet the IRS has no institutional memory that we were ever there. It's too early to tell what the impact of all this activity will be, but it would be a mistake to dismiss the movement."

Questions About the Reading

1. According to the article, what percentage of companies with 500 or more employees have ethics programs?
2. What was the initial cause for the establishment of the ethics programs?
3. What are the ethical violations described in paragraph 4 of the article?
4. What is the training process used for the ethical program at Lockheed Martin?
5. What caused Bell Atlantic to become interested in ethics programs for public schools?

Thinking Critically

1. Do you think schools should offer programs teaching ethics and values? Why or why not?
2. What would you do if you knew a classmate was turning in a composition that was taken from the Internet?
3. Would you be willing to participate in an ethics program offered by your employer or would you resent having to attend the program?

Writing Assignments

1. Write a memo to the director of human resources of your company expressing your reaction to the company-sponsored ethics program that you attended.
2. Assume that you want your company to offer an ethics program. Find out which companies in your town offer ethics programs for their employees. Write an informal report describing the companies, the programs, and the curriculum of the programs. Write a letter transmitting the report to the president of your company, Cyberspace.com.

5

Time Management, Problem Solving, and Decision Making

IT IS SOMETIMES said that if you want something done, ask someone who is busy. But can you be too busy? And are you too busy because you are not managing your time efficiently? In "The Cult of Busyness," Barbara Ehrenreich says that "busyness" has become a new value, especially among professional women but also for men. Edwin Bliss provides us with advice for using our time more wisely in "Managing Your Time."

Problem solving is something you need to be able to do in both your work and your personal life. In "How Not to Lose Friends over Money," Lois Duncan suggests ways to solve problems you might have involving loans to friends and colleagues at work. In "Putting a Lid on Conflicts," Michael Barrier provides examples of how various businesses have handled workplace conflicts.

Like problem solving, decision making is something you need to be able to do in both your personal life and your work. In "It's Time to Make up Your Mind," Winston Fletcher offers some practical suggestions for overcoming indecisiveness and making difficult decisions. The possible consequences of choosing one's personal ethics over the actions or standards of the workplace are explained by Geanne Rosenberg in "Truth or Consequences," along with advice from human resources professionals on how to handle such conflicting choices.

In this chapter you will be asked to keep a time log and to follow a process in solving a problem and making a decision.

The Time Log

A time log is a daily record of all your activities and the amount of time you spent on each. Most people feel they do not have enough time for everything they have to do and want to do. After they have kept a daily time log for a week or two, however, they realize that they can use their time more efficiently. On page 115 is an example of a time log kept for one day.

If the same pattern of activities continues every day through the week, the person keeping this activity log would have spent fifteen and three-quarter hours talking on the telephone, checking and responding to e-mail, and playing computer games during the day. By reducing each of those activities to fifteen minutes a day, the person would gain forty-five minutes a day and five and one-quarter hours over the week to spend in other, probably more productive activities.

Problem Solving

Suppose, for example, that you observe a worker disposing of waste products improperly and in violation of environmental requirements. You need to recognize, first, that this activity is a problem and decide to solve it. The problem-solving process involves the following steps:

1. Defining the problem (disposing of waste products improperly)
2. Finding the cause of the problem
3. Listing possible solutions
4. Choosing a solution
5. Implementing the solution
6. Evaluating the solution

Finding the cause of the problem may involve talking to the worker to find out why he or she is disposing of waste improperly. He or she may be negligent or unaware of the proper procedures. Once the cause is known, a solution can be chosen. For example, if the cause is negligence, the worker could be advised and warned that the proper procedures must be followed. If the cause is lack of knowledge, the worker should be taught the proper procedures. The appropriate solution must then be implemented. Through observation of the worker, you can then determine that the proper procedures are being followed.

Decision Making

Suppose you have an opportunity to take a different job with your company. The new job is at an increased salary but requires that you move to

Activity

Time	Activity	Time	Activity
7:00	Got up, brushed	**1:00**	Went to lunch.
:15	teeth, etc.	:15	
:30	Dressed.	:30	
:45	Made coffee and ate	:45	Went to 2nd class.
8:00	breakfast.	**2:00**	In class.
:15	Read paper.	:15	
:30	Read paper.	:30	
:45	Answered phone.	:45	Left class for home.
9:00	Talked to friend.	**3:00**	
:15	" " "	:15	
:30	Went for walk.	:30	Arrived home.
:45	" " "	:45	Played computer
10:00	" " "	**4:00**	games.
:15	Checked for e-mail.	:15	
:30	Answered e-mail.	:30	Went to grocery.
:45	" " "	:45	
11:00	Left for school.	**5:00**	
:15		:15	
:30		:30	Home from grocery.
:45	Arrived at school.	:45	
12:00	Went to class.	**6:00**	Fixed dinner.
:15		:15	Ate dinner.
:30		:30	
:45	Left 1st class.	:45	Watched TV.

another city. Among the many factors you would need to consider are the cost of moving, housing costs in the new city, and personal and family concerns. Listing the pros and cons, or advantages and disadvantages, of taking the new job can help you make your decision, as in the following example:

Pros	Cons
Increased income	Moving costs
Better housing	Increased housing costs
Increased responsibility	More time at work
Better schools	Leaving family and friends
Chance for advancement	Anxiety about newly created position

When you weigh the increased income against the increased costs, you may find that you may not be better off financially in the new position. You may feel, however, that the chance for advancement outweighs the insecurity of the newly created position. Your family may be upset by the move. What would you decide about taking the position?

The Cult of Busyness

Barbara Ehrenreich

In this excerpt from her book The Worst Years of Our Lives: Irreverent Notes from a Decade of Greed, *Barbara Ehrenreich addresses "busyness," which she says has become a new value in our society.*

Before You Read

How do you manage your time?

Words to Know

acumen   judgment, wisdom
dispersion   wide distribution, scattering
ingestion   taking in, eating
insignia   sign, mark
tribulations   sufferings, distresses

Not too long ago a former friend and soon-to-be acquaintance called 1 me up to tell me how busy she was. A major report, upon which her professional future depended, was due in three days; her secretary was on strike; her housekeeper had fallen into the hands of the Immigration Department; she had two hours to prepare a dinner party for eight; and she was late for her time-management class. Stress was taking its toll, she told me: her children resented the fact that she sometimes got their names mixed up, and she had taken to abusing white wine.

All this put me at a distinct disadvantage, since the only thing I was 2 doing at the time was holding the phone with one hand and attempting to touch the opposite toe with the other hand, a pastime that I had perfected during previous telephone monologues. Not that I'm not busy too: as I listened to her, I was on the alert for the moment the dryer would shut itself off and I would have to rush to fold the clothes before they settled into a mass of incorrigible wrinkles. But if I mentioned this little deadline of mine, she might think I wasn't busy enough to need a housekeeper, so I just kept on patiently saying "Hmm" until she got to her parting line: "Look, this isn't a good time for me to talk, I've got to go now."

I don't know when the cult of conspicuous busyness began, but it has 3 swept up almost all the upwardly mobile, professional women I know. Already, it is getting hard to recall the days when, for example "Let's

117

have lunch" meant something other than "I've got more important things to do than talk to you right now." There was even a time when people used to get together without the excuse of needing something to eat— when, in fact, it was considered rude to talk with your mouth full. In the old days, hardly anybody had an appointment book, and when people wanted to know what the day held in store for them, they consulted a horoscope.

It's not only women, of course; for both sexes, busyness has become an 4 important insignia of upper-middle-class status. Nobody, these days, admits to having a hobby, although two or more careers—say, neurosurgery and an art dealership—is not uncommon, and I am sure we will soon be hearing more about the tribulations of the four-paycheck couple. Even those who can manage only one occupation at a time would be embarrassed to be caught doing only one *thing* at a time. Those young men who jog with their headsets on are not, as you might innocently guess, rocking out, but are absorbing the principles of international finance law or a lecture on one-minute management. Even eating, I read recently, is giving way to "grazing"—the conscious ingestion of unidentified foods while drafting a legal brief, cajoling a client on the phone, and, in ambitious cases, doing calf-toning exercises under the desk.

But for women, there's more at stake than conforming to another up- 5 scale standard. If you want to attract men, for example, it no longer helps to be a bimbo with time on your hands. Upscale young men seem to go for the kind of woman who plays with a full deck of credit cards, who won't cry when she's knocked to the ground while trying to board the six o'clock Eastern shuttle. . . . Then there is the economic reality: any woman who doesn't want to wind up a case study in the feminization of poverty has to be successful at something more demanding than fingernail maintenance or come-hither looks. Hence all the bustle, my busy friends would explain—they want to succeed.

But if success is the goal, it seems clear to me that the fast track is headed 6 the wrong way. Think of the people who are genuinely successful—pathbreaking scientists, best-selling novelists, and designers of major new software. They are not, on the whole, the kind of people who keep glancing shiftily at their watches or making small lists entitled "To Do." On the contrary, many of these people appear to be in a daze, like the distinguished professor I once had who, in the middle of a lecture on electron spin, became so fascinated by the dispersion properties of chalk dust that he could not go on. These truly successful people are childlike, easily distractable, fey sorts, whose usual demeanor resembles that of a recently fed hobo on a warm summer evening.

The secret of the truly successful, I believe, is that they learned very 7 early in life how *not* to be busy. They saw through that adage, repeated to me so often in childhood, that anything worth doing is worth doing well. The truth is, many things are worth doing only in the most slovenly, half-hearted fashion possible, and many other things are not worth doing at all. Balancing a checkbook, for example. For some reason, in our culture, this dreary exercise is regarded as the supreme test of personal maturity, business acumen, and the ability to cope with math anxiety. Yet it is a form of busyness which is exceeded in futility only by going to the additional trouble of computerizing one's checking account—and that, in turn, is only slightly less silly than taking the time to discuss, with anyone, what brand of personal computer one owns, or is thinking of buying, or has heard of others using.

If the truly successful manage never to be busy, it is also true that many   8 of the busiest people will never be successful. I know this firsthand from my experience, many years ago, as a waitress. Any executive who thinks the ultimate in busyness consists of having two important phone calls on hold and a major deadline in twenty minutes, should try facing six tablefuls of clients simultaneously demanding that you give them their checks, fresh coffee, a baby seat, and a warm, spontaneous smile. Even when she's not busy, a waitress has to look busy—refilling the salt shakers and polishing all the chrome in sight—but the only reward is the minimum wage and any change that gets left on the tables. Much the same is true of other high-stress jobs, like working as a telephone operator, or doing data entry on one of the new machines that monitors your speed as you work: "success" means surviving the shift.

Although busyness does not lead to success, I am willing to believe   9 that success—especially when visited on the unprepared—can cause busyness. Anyone who has invented a better mousetrap, or the contemporary equivalent, can expect to be harassed by strangers demanding that you read their unpublished manuscripts or undergo the humiliation of public speaking, usually on remote Midwestern campuses. But if it is true that success leads to more busyness and less time for worthwhile activities—like talking (and listening) to friends, reading novels, or putting in some volunteer time for a good cause—then who needs it? It would be sad to have come so far—or at least to have run so hard—only to lose each other.

Questions About the Reading

1. What does the writer mean by referring to her caller as "a former friend and soon-to-be acquaintance"?
2. What was the writer doing while talking on the telephone? Why did she stay on the telephone with the caller?

3. What does the writer mean when she says that genuinely successful people have learned how not to be busy?
4. What is the writer's opinion of balancing one's checkbook and computerizing one's checking account? Do you agree?

Thinking Critically

1. What are the absolutely essential tasks that you should accomplish each day? How much time do you need for each?
2. What did you do yesterday and how much time did you spend on each activity? Which of the activities do you think was a waste of time, which do you think you could have done in less time, and which do you think you needed to spend more time on?

Writing Assignments

1. In your journal, develop a schedule of all your daytime activities for the next seven days.
2. Using your schedule for the next seven days, develop a time log that includes each of the daytime activities.

Managing Your Time

Edwin Bliss

There is never enough time to do what we have to do. But Edwin Bliss, a management consultant, tells us how to make more time by using the time we have wisely. Bliss offers ten simple steps. You can use any or all of them, in any order.

Before You Read

Do you plan your day's activities ahead of time or tackle what comes up?

Words to Know

adversely badly, negatively
allocate set apart for a specific purpose
attainable reachable
chaotic confused and disordered
constituents the residents of a certain voting area
differentiate note the difference between items
disservice harm
irretrievably not capable of being recovered
subordinate one who is lower in rank or status
tactfully done or said in a way that avoids offending or hurting

---

1 I first became interested in the effective use of time when I was an assistant to a U.S. Senator. Members of Congress are faced with urgent and conflicting demands on their time—for committee work, floor votes, speeches, interviews, briefings, correspondence, investigations, constituents' problems, and the need to be informed on a wide range of subjects. The more successful Congressmen develop techniques for getting maximum benefit from minimum investments of time. If they don't, they don't return.

2 Realizing that I was not one of those who use time effectively, I began to apply in my own life some of the techniques I had observed. Here are ten I have found most helpful.

3 **Plan.** You need a game plan for your day. Otherwise, you'll allocate your time according to whatever happens to land on your desk. And you will find yourself making the fatal mistake of dealing primarily with prob-

lems rather than opportunities. Start each day by making a general schedule, with particular emphasis on the two or three major things you would
like to accomplish—including things that will achieve long-term goals.
Remember, studies prove what common sense tells us: the more time we
spend planning a project, the less total time is required for it. Don't let
today's busywork crowd planning-time out of your schedule.

Concentrate. Of all the principles of time management, none is more 4
basic than concentration. People who have serious time-management
problems invariably are trying to do too many things at once. The amount
of time spent on a project is not what counts: it's the amount of *uninter-
rupted* time. Few problems can resist an all-out attack; few can be solved
piecemeal.

Take Breaks. To work for long periods without taking a break is not 5
an effective use of time. Energy decreases, boredom sets in, and physical
stress and tension accumulate. Switching for a few minutes from a mental task to something physical—isometric exercises, walking around the
office, even changing from a sitting position to a standing position for a
while—can provide relief.

Merely resting, however, is often the best course, and you should not 6
think of a "rest" break as poor use of time. Not only will being refreshed
increase your efficiency, but relieving tension will benefit your health.
Anything that contributes to health is good time management.

Avoid Clutter. Some people have a constant swirl of papers on their 7
desks and assume that somehow the most important matters will float to
the top. In most cases, however, clutter hinders concentration and can
create tension and frustration—a feeling of being "snowed under."

Whenever you find your desk becoming chaotic, take time out to reor- 8
ganize. Go through all your papers (making generous use of the wastebasket) and divide them into categories: (1) Immediate action, (2) Low
priority, (3) Pending, (4) Reading material. Put the highest priority item
from your first pile in the center of your desk, then put everything else
out of sight. Remember, you can think of only one thing at a time, and
you can work on only one task at a time, so focus all your attention on the
most important one. A final point: clearing the desk completely, or at least
organizing it, each evening should be standard practice. It gets the next
day off to a good start.

Don't Be a Perfectionist. There is a difference between striving for 9
excellence and striving for perfection. The first is attainable, gratifying
and healthy. The second is often unattainable, frustrating and neurotic.
It's also a terrible waste of time. The stenographer who retypes a lengthy
letter because of a trivial error, or the boss who demands such retyping,
might profit from examining the Declaration of Independence. When the
inscriber of that document made two errors of omission, he inserted the

missing letters between the lines. If this is acceptable in the document that gave birth to American freedom, surely it would be acceptable in a letter that will be briefly glanced at en route to someone's file cabinet or wastebasket!

Don't Be Afraid to Say No. Of all the time-saving techniques ever 10 developed, perhaps the most effective is frequent use of the word *no.* Learn to decline, tactfully but firmly, every request that does not contribute to your goals. If you point out that your motivation is not to get out of work but to save your time to do a better job on the really important things, you'll have a good chance of avoiding unproductive tasks. Remember, many people who worry about offending others wind up living according to other people's priorities.

Don't Procrastinate. Procrastination is usually a deeply rooted habit. 11 But we can change our habits provided we use the right system. William James, the father of American psychology, discussed such a system in his famous *Principles of Psychology*, published in 1890. It works as follows:

1. Decide to start changing as soon as you finish reading this article, while you are motivated. Taking that first step promptly is important.
2. Don't try to do too much too quickly. Just force yourself right now to do one thing you have been putting off. Then, beginning tomorrow morning, start each day by doing the most unpleasant thing on your schedule. Often it will be a small matter: an overdue apology; a confrontation with a fellow worker; an annoying chore you know you should tackle. Whatever it is, do it before you begin your usual morning routine. This simple procedure can well set the tone for your day. You will get a feeling of exhilaration from knowing that although the day is only 15 minutes old, you have already accomplished the most unpleasant thing you have to do all day.

There is one caution, however: Do not permit any exceptions. William 12 James compared it to rolling up a ball of string; a single slip can undo more than many turns can wind up. Be tough with yourself, for the first few minutes of each day, for the next two weeks, and I promise you a new habit of priceless value.

Apply Radical Surgery. Time-wasting activities are like cancers. They 13 drain off vitality and have a tendency to grow. The only cure is radical surgery. If you are wasting your time in activities that bore you, divert you from your real goals and sap your energy, cut them out, once and for all.

The principle applies to personal habits, routines, and activities as much 14 as to ones associated with your work. Check your appointment calendar, your extracurricular activities, your reading list, your television viewing habits, and ax everything that doesn't give you a feeling of accomplishment or satisfaction.

Delegate. An early example of failure to delegate is found in the Bible. 15
Moses, having led his people out of Egypt, was so impressed with his
own knowledge and authority that he insisted on ruling personally on
every controversy that arose in Israel. His wise father-in-law, Jethro, recognizing that this was poor use of a leader's time, recommended a two-
phase approach: first, educate the people concerning the laws; second,
select capable leaders and give them full authority over routine matters,
freeing Moses to concentrate on major decisions. The advice is still sound.

You don't have to be a national leader or a corporate executive to del- 16
egate, either. Parents who don't delegate household chores are doing a
disservice to themselves and their children. Running a Boy Scout troop
can be as time-consuming as running General Motors if you try to do
everything yourself. One caution: giving subordinates jobs that neither
you nor anyone else wants to do isn't delegating, it's assigning. Learn to
delegate the challenging and rewarding tasks, along with sufficient authority to make necessary decisions. It can help to free your time.

Don't Be a "Workaholic." Most successful executives I know work 17
long hours, but they don't let work interfere with the really important
things in life, such as friends, family, and fly fishing. This differentiates
them from the workaholic who becomes addicted to work just as people
become addicted to alcohol. Symptoms of work addiction include refusal
to take a vacation, inability to put the office out of your mind on weekends, a bulging briefcase, and a wife, son, or daughter who is practically
a stranger.

Counseling can help people cope with such problems. But for starters, 18
do a bit of self-counseling. Ask yourself whether the midnight oil you are
burning is adversely affecting your health. Ask where your family comes
in your list of priorities, whether you are giving enough of yourself to
your children and spouse, and whether you are deceiving yourself by
pretending that the sacrifices you are making are really for them.

Above all else, good time management involves an awareness that to- 19
day is all we ever have to work with. The past is irretrievably gone, the
future is only a concept. British art critic John Ruskin had the word
"TODAY" carved into a small marble block that he kept on his desk as a
constant reminder to "Do It Now." But my favorite quotation is by an
anonymous philosopher:

> Yesterday is a canceled check.
> Tomorrow is a promissory note.
> Today is ready cash. Use it!

Questions About the Reading

1. What was the work the writer was doing when he became interested in the effective use of time?
2. What are the ten steps for effective time management?
3. Which time-saving technique does the writer say is perhaps the most effective?

Thinking Critically

1. Which of the time management techniques described by the writer do you practice? Which do you need to work on to make more effective use of your time?
2. Which profession do you think requires the most effective time management skills: doctor, lawyer, business executive, teacher? Why?

Writing Assignments

1. In your journal, plan your schedule for the next five days. Include all your activities, errands, class attendance, and at least one special thing you expect to accomplish each day.
2. Make a time log to correspond to the schedules you planned for the next five days.

How Not to Lose Friends over Money

Lois Duncan

Perhaps you have had a problem with a friend involving money. Lois Duncan provides ten examples of situations you may have experienced and suggests how each situation can be handled without losing a friend.

Before You Read

Have you ever felt that a friend took advantage of you financially?

Words to Know

impasse   dead end, dilemma
profusely   abundantly, freely
reciprocation   return, exchange
reimbursed   paid back, compensated
shyster   unethical or unscrupulous person

When I was in the third grade, a girl named Olivia borrowed money   1
from me to buy a Coke. She never paid it back. I was too embarrassed to
ask for it. I didn't want my friend to think I didn't trust her.

One day Olivia was absent from school. She had moved to Philadel-   2
phia, and my money had gone with her. I was outraged!

Many years later, I am still outraged. I wake in the night with the feel   3
of Olivia's throat in my hands! Surpassing my fury, however, is contempt
for my eight-year-old self because I did not stand up to that pigtailed
shyster and demand what was mine.

I'd like to say that the experience taught me a lesson. But the sad truth   4
is I still have problems with friends and money. Almost everyone I know
has similar difficulties. The stickiest situations seem to be those in which
the amounts are so small that it doesn't seem worth the risk of alienating
a friend to make a fuss. At the same time, we all resent being treated
unfairly, and our buried hostility often threatens the very friendship we
are struggling so hard to preserve.

As Dr. Signey Rosenblum, professor of psychology and psychiatry at   5
the University of New Mexico, explains, "Money is important not just for
what it can buy, but for what it may symbolize—power, social status,
even love. When a friend takes advantage of us financially, it is hard to be

objective. Subconsciously, we get the message that we are not important enough to that person to merit fair treatment."

What seems fair to one person, however, often seems totally unfair to another. A candid discussion may help, but differences in values cannot always be resolved. In some cases, you simply have to decide how much a friendship is worth—and act accordingly. But most of these problems can be handled successfully—sometimes with surprising ease.   6

I consulted psychologists and counselors on this issue, but found that some of the best advice came from women who had learned to cope through trial and error. Here are their solutions to ten common money problems that come between friends: 7

1. A companion suggests splitting a restaurant tab in half when her share is much larger than yours. Randy and Sally get together for a long, gossipy lunch at least once a month. Randy, who is perennially on a diet, always orders a salad and coffee, while skinny Sally goes for broke with veal scallopini and a lavish dessert. Many times, she also has a glass or two of wine. When the bill arrives, Sally always says, "Let's just split it, OK?" Although Randy's meal usually costs about a third of Sally's, she's reluctant to appear cheap.   8

"I used to tell myself that such inequities even out in the long run," Randy says, "but they *don't*. The person who orders the most expensive dish on the menu one day is usually the one who does it the next time too."   9

Her solution is a pocket calculator. "Before Sally can suggest going halfsies," she says, "I offer to do the accounting. I tell her I love to use this nifty gadget my husband gave me for my birthday. Then I do a quick calculation and plunk down cash to cover my share; Sally pays the rest. She's never complained so maybe she just hates to do arithmetic."   10

2. You become involved in an unequal gift exchange. Nobody expects the presents she receives to cost exactly the same as those she gives, but a wide disparity is embarrassing for both parties. Some women avoid this problem by getting friends to agree on a maximum amount in advance. This can only work, however, when the gift exchange is an established tradition.   11

"The most distressing situations occur when you're taken by surprise," says Reneé, a schoolteacher. "The day school let out for Christmas, a colleague stopped me to say she had a little gift for me in her car. I had nothing for her, so I rushed out and bought her a pair of lovely earrings on my lunch hour. Her present turned out to be a dime-store joke gift. She thanked me profusely for the earrings, but it was obvious that she was embarrassed—and so was I."   12

If this were to happen again, Reneé says she'd open the package before deciding on an appropriate form of reciprocation. "I might not give a   13 present at all," she says. "Instead, I could invite her over for eggnog during the holidays or ask her to be my guest at a Christmas program. Every gesture of friendship doesn't have to be repaid in kind."

Many other women agreed. Said one: "I think people should give what 14 they want to and can afford—without worrying overmuch about equality of cost. When you're hung up on monetary value, you're not *giving*, you're *trading*. If you're going to do that, you might just as well exchange checks for equal amounts."

3. A passenger in your car neglects to pay her share of expenses. 15 "When Amy and I took a long trip in my car," says Phyllis, "I just assumed we'd each pay half. Amy did her part as she saw it, paying for every other tank of gas. But when the radiator hose burst in Salt Lake City, I paid for the replacement. When the fuel pump went out in Chicago, I paid for repairs. The cost of a tune-up and oil change before the trip and the car wash when we got back—I absorbed them all."

Phyllis realizes that she was partly to blame for not discussing finances 16 in advance, but will not make the same mistake again. "When I use my own car for business," she says, "I get reimbursed twenty cents a mile. So the next time I furnish transportation for a pleasure trip, I'll make it clear from the start that I expect my companion to contribute ten cents a mile."

A more common problem arises when one person provides regular 17 chauffeur service for a friend who never chips in for gas. "I don't think most nondrivers mean to take advantage," one woman said; "they just don't realize how much it costs to operate a car. One day I pulled into a self-service station and asked my friend to finish filling the tank while I dashed to the ladies room. By the time I got back, she was staring in horror at the price gauge and fishing for her wallet."

4. You are given a check that bounces. When Roberta went out to 18 dinner and the theater with a friend from out of town, she paid both bills with her credit card. Lisa then paid for her share of the evening's expenses by giving Roberta a check—one that later bounced.

"It was very awkward," Roberta recalls. "I considered absorbing the 19 whole cost of the evening myself just to avoid embarrassing Lisa. I knew, though, that if I did I'd always feel resentful. Our friendship would be bound to suffer—and Lisa wouldn't even know why."

Roberta handled the situation by sending Lisa the bounced check, along 20 with a lighthearted note saying, "If your bank is like mine, they botched up your account. Shall we try again?" Lisa responded with a note of apology and another check—one that cleared—and the incident was never referred to by either woman again.

5. A friend invites you to participate in an activity that costs more 21 than you can afford—or want—to spend. "When my college roommate asked me to be matron-of-honor at her wedding, I was flattered," Louise recalls. "My immediate response was, 'I'd love to!' After I hung up, however, I began to realize how much expense was involved. The dress had to be specially made, with new shoes dyed to match—and the wedding was halfway across the country. My husband and I were saving to go to Europe and couldn't afford to do both."

Louise decided to be honest. "I called her back and explained the situ- 22 ation," she says. "My roommate was hurt, of course, and I felt bad about that. But I'd have felt even worse if I'd sacrificed the trip I'd been looking forward to for so long."

Not everyone I polled agreed with this approach. All thought Louise 23 had been right to turn down the invitation, but some felt she could have done it more kindly. "She might have said that previous plans made it impossible for her to attend the wedding," one woman suggested. "She didn't have to explain that the plans were for a trip to Europe. In Louise's place, I'd have tried to spare my friend's feelings by not mentioning that this milestone in her life was not nearly as important to me as it was to her."

6. You are asked to contribute toward a gift for someone you don't 24 **know well or don't like.** "Every week it seems," says Eileen, "I'm asked to make a contribution toward another gift or a party to celebrate somebody's new baby, birthday, or retirement. I resent forking over money for people I hardly know, but how do you get out of it when everybody else is doing it?"

The simplest solution: just say no. "It doesn't sound that bad if you do 25 it regretfully," one woman suggests. "'I wish I could contribute,' I'd say, 'but it just isn't possible.'"

Another friend handles this problem differently. "If the honored per- 26 son is somebody I'd be buying for anyway," she explains, "I donate the amount I'd have spent myself. If it's someone I know only slightly, I give a few coins as a token. What I *don't* do is apologize for my contribution— or let myself be pressured into giving more than I feel is really appropriate."

7. A friend is able to spend far more—or far less—than you can. We 27 don't choose friends on the basis of how much money they have, of course, but vast differences can be disturbing to both sides. Erin, for example, is single and earns a very good salary. Her friend Pat, a divorced mother of three, is struggling to make ends meet.

"We're both theater buffs," Erin explains. "And I'd gladly pay for two 28 tickets just to have Pat's company at plays and concerts. But she won't go anywhere unless she can pay her own way. I hate to go alone, so we both stay home. It all seems so silly."

Pat sees the situation differently. "After an unhappy marriage to a domi- 29
neering man," she says, "it's very important to me to carry my own weight.
I'm not comfortable in any relationship where all I do is take."

The impasse was finally broken when Erin moved recently. Pat's chil- 30
dren were with their father so she took a picnic lunch to her friend's new
place, then spent the day helping her unpack and get settled. "I was so
grateful," Erin says, "that I persuaded Pat to let me return the favor in
my own way—with season tickets to our little theater group. I think she
is beginning to recognize that she contributes as much to our friendship
as I do."

8. Social pressure forces you to overspend. "When you're out with a 31
group, weird things can happen to common sense," says Valerie. "For
example, my husband and I often meet after work on Fridays at a club
we belong to. We always run into people we know there, and inevitably
somebody snatches the bar tab and says, 'I'll get this round; you can get
the next one.' That seems fair on the surface, but a single beer is my
husband's limit and I drink club soda. More often than not, we find ourselves hosting a round of double martinis for casual acquaintances."

After several such occasions, Valerie and her husband agreed to refuse 32
to be shoved into "picking up a round" again. "Now when a second batch
of drinks is ordered, we just insist, 'No more for us, thanks,'" Valerie
says. "We don't make excuses or offer prolonged explanations. If the person who paid for he first round gets upset, that's *his* problem. *Ours* is
solved!"

9. A friend asks personal questions about your finances. "Some 33
people don't seem to mind being asked how much they earn or what
they spend for their clothes, but I am offended by such questions," says
Heather. "To my way of thinking, our finances are nobody else's business. Yet when we were first married, a nosy acquaintance asked what
my husband's salary was and I was so startled I actually *told* her!"

In the years since, Heather has developed techniques for putting money 34
snoops in their place. "It's a state secret," she tells them, or "I can't remember what I paid." Today, if someone is crass enough to ask about her
husband's salary, she responds with questions of her own: "Why do you
care about that? Are you planning to apply for his job?"

10. A companion borrows money and "forgets" to repay it. Large loans 35
are seldom the issue; they're usually treated as business transactions, with
the terms spelled out on paper. But many women suffer in silence over
problems like Carol's. "My friend Ginny is always short of cash," she
says. "I hate to recall how often I've 'loaned' her a dollar or two for a
drink or a movie. Each loan is so small I'd feel really cheap making a big
deal of it; still, I *do* resent the fact that she never pays me back."

Carol admits to being "too inhibited or something" to demand repay- 36 ment, but she has resolved to stop giving money to Ginny. "The last time she asked for five dollars to pay for her dry cleaning, I just told her I couldn't spare it."

Another woman suggests a gutsier response. "When somebody cops 37 out on repaying a loan, I turn the tables by requesting one myself," she says. "'I left home without my wallet,' I'll say. 'Can you lend me enough to cover lunch?' Then, when the money is safely in hand, I am struck by a sudden realization. 'Why, this is exactly the amount I loaned you last week! How convenient! Now you won't have to repay me!'" She says it works like a charm.

Then, there's the *really* gutsy solution in which we simply ask, straight 38 out, in no-nonsense language, for what is rightfully ours. This, I've come to realize, is what I should have done with Olivia. If I were to run into her today, I like to think I'd have the strength of character to step right up and say, "Olivia, I have an overwhelming desire for a soda. How about giving me the cash I loaned you forty years ago?"

If she did hand it over, I think I might forgive her and renew our friend- 39 ship—despite the fact that you can no longer buy a Coke with a dime!

Questions About the Reading

1. What was the writer's first experience with loaning money to a friend?
2. What are the "stickiest situations" the writer faces related to friends and money?
3. How did Randy solve the problem of splitting a restaurant tab in half?
4. How did Roberta handle the bounced check she received from her friend?
5. What does the writer realize she should have done about the money she loaned to a friend?

Thinking Critically

1. How would you respond if a fellow worker asked you to cosign a note for a bank loan?
2. What would you do if you were asked to contribute more than you can afford to a gift for a coworker?

Writing Assignments

1. Suppose your closest friend is accused of taking money from her company and is on trial. She asks you to commit perjury to defend her from the charges. Using the problem-solving process explained on page 114, write an essay explaining what you would do.
2. Suppose you are offered two identical jobs, except that one is in another state and you would have to relocate. Using the problem-solving process, write an essay explaining how you would choose between the two jobs.

Putting a Lid on Conflicts

Michael Barrier

In this article, Michael Barrier stresses the importance of managing, not suppressing, employee conflicts and establishing rules governing conflict in the workplace.

Before You Read

If you managed a business, what rules would you establish for handling conflicts?

Words to Know

entrepreneurs   organizers of a business

insidious   dangerous, treacherous

obligation   debt, responsibility

perspective   viewpoint

It's the horrific stories of workplace violence that catch your eye—the 1
postal worker who murders his colleagues, or the fired employee who returns to kill the boss he blames. For many small businesses, however, the danger is not from that kind of extreme violence, but from lower levels of internal conflict. A company can be slowly poisoned by anger and hostility.

"In large companies," says Dennis A. Davis, a San Diego consultant 2
and the author of *Threats Pending, Fuses Burning: Managing Workplace Violence . . .* , "it is possible to still be anonymous except to those people who work immediately around you. In a small company, that just isn't possible.

"The presence of conflict and tension in a small company, even if it's 3
just between two individuals, has much larger ramifications for the company as a whole. You can't avoid knowing what's going on in a small company."

When Donna Stringer and a business partner started a Seattle-based 4
training company, Executive Diversity Services (EDS), in 1989, they tried to head off internal conflicts by deciding what "core behaviors" they wanted from their employees before the company ever opened its doors.

Only four people—Stringer, her partner, and two other consultants— 5
worked at EDS then, and the company is still small. It has only seven full-time staff members, along with dozens of trainers who work as indepen-

dent contractors in other cities. But even so manageable a growth rate became an incubator for conflict.

As the company grew and began to serve larger clients, Stringer says, 6 its owners failed to re-examine those "core expectations" and say, "Are they still serving us?"—even though growth meant that "people had to do different kinds of things in different ways."

As EDS added people—a business manager, a client-services manager, 7 a marketing manager—to the original four, Stringer says, "[T]he four of us continued acting the way we used to act. If the phone rings and it's a potential marketing contact, you handle it. If a client wants some material modified, you do it. So the four of us were getting in the way of other people doing the things they'd been hired to do.

"Scheduling was a big issue," she continues. "The phone rings, some- 8 body wants training on a certain day, and I look at the calendar and say, 'Sure, that day's free, we'll schedule you in there.' What I don't know is that the business manager is on the phone talking to somebody else [about training on the same date], and it's her responsibility to schedule. So I just screwed up."

It's hard, though, to tell the president of the company that she has just 9 made a mess of things. "What you do," Stringer says, "is fuss and fume and talk to somebody else about it, and pretty soon everybody's all riled up."

Such conflict among the people working in a small firm can be insidi- 10 ous because business owners and managers recoil from doing what's needed to control it. "Entrepreneurs have to be very task-focused, goal-oriented," says Charles E. Labig, a Chicago-based corporate psychologist and the author of *Preventing Violence in the Workplace*. . . . "That set of skills tends not to go along with human-relations skills."

Says Stringer: "The top two things that managers tell us they don't 11 want to deal with are conflict resolution and performance evaluation—and they don't like performance evaluation because it can cause conflict."

Fortunately, there are some relatively simple steps that a small- 12 business owner can take to keep conflict under control. Among them:

Manage conflict—don't suppress it. Small-business owners and man- 13 agers should regard conflict not as an evil to be eliminated, the experts suggest, but as an inevitable phenomenon to be managed to the company's benefit.

"Good management brings out differences of opinion, to see all sides 14 and come to the best decision," says Labig, who worked in Boston for a dozen years as an independent consultant to family-owned businesses and partnerships. Daniel S. Hanson, author of *Cultivating Common Ground: Releasing the Power of Relationships at Work* . . . , calls conflict "an opportunity to gain knowledge."

Even though EDS is itself a training organization, it now tries to bring 15 conflicts to the surface by calling in outside trainers twice a year. "Every time we bring somebody in to do some teamwork with us or communications work with us," Stringer says, "we discover something else that one of us has been troubled by and hasn't necessarily been talking about."

Training is hardly a cure-all, however. "Intuitively," Hanson says, "as 16 a manager, I think you know if a group is stuck in deep, bad conflict or they're just having difficulty working on surface issues." In the latter case, formal training may be overkill, and an honest group discussion is all that's needed.

Whatever you do, don't try to suppress conflict by discouraging ex- 17 pressions of disagreement. What usually happens when companies try to suppress conflict, Hanson says, "is that it comes out in odd places and in odd ways—as workplace violence if it gets really bad, or as unproductive activity behind the scenes," such as constant griping.

Establish clear rules governing conflicts. As Labig says, "It's the job 18 of senior management to create the environment of an organization"— and that job includes laying down rules governing disagreements. "That means you have rules for how you treat each other; you have rules about listening, about being respectful, and about trying to appreciate the differences in style and perspective."

Supervisors must be "very clear" about the behavior they expect, 19 Stringer says, adopting a "preventive strategy" that entails "identifying as clearly and overtly as possible what behaviors will and will not be tolerated in the work environment."

Such rules should mandate "a focus on the issue and not on the per- 20 son," says San Diego consultant Davis. The rules should mark out prohibited behaviors, including violence and threats of violence, but they also "should encourage the resolution of conflict through discussion."

One small example of a successful rule: Hanson, an executive of Land 21 O'Lakes Inc. in Arden Hills, Minn., works with a team of six executives, and, he says, "[W]e say that we will not attack someone until we have repeated what they've said to their satisfaction." Disagreement is thus focused clearly on the other person's position.

Even though employers should write the rules, they should be open to 22 changing those rules in response to employee feedback. "What's important," Hanson says, "is to get to the point where the entire group has some input into what the codes of behavior are."

American workers demand not the freedom to do whatever they wish, 23 Davis says, but the courtesy of explanations for what they are required to do.

Make your own behavior a model. Setting clear rules isn't enough; 24 it's just as important that you obey them. "Where you get into problems is when senior management doesn't live by its own rules," Labig says.

If a boss tells employees to treat one another with respect but treats 25
them with obvious contempt, employees will ignore the words and follow the example. "How the owner models behavior is a critical element,"
Labig says. "If I run the business and I beat up somebody emotionally in
front of everybody else, you're going to see that ripple through the whole
company."

You may want someone to tug on your sleeve when you need remind- 26
ing of your obligation to set an example. "A lot of smart entrepreneurs
have someone working with them, either within the organization or as a
mentor or a coach, to help them deal with the interpersonal side," says
Hanson.

Avoid ending up with winners and losers. Resolving disagreements, 27
Stringer suggests, shouldn't be a matter of "figuring out who's right and
who's wrong" but of deciding which outcome "is going to most effectively serve the business."

Inevitably, though, if an employee's point of view does not prevail—if 28
in particular you as a boss reject the employee's idea—the employee will
feel like a loser. But what is likely to matter most to the employee, Davis
says, is not that he or she lost "but that you were respectful and courte-
ous, and it seemed that [the employee's] opinion counted for something.
That's what's crucial. How it's done is more significant than what's done."

Labig agrees: "The human factor is critical. It's not just getting to a 29
decision; it's helping the group form the kind of team that is going to
maximize profitability for the company."

As Davis puts it, the way to manage conflict well is to bring each em- 30
ployee around "to genuinely caring about what's best for the company,
even if my idea isn't it."

Questions About the Reading

1. What is the main idea of the article?
2. What are the steps small-business owners and managers can take to
   manage employee conflict?
3. What example of a successful rule does the writer give? (See paragraph 21.)

Thinking Critically

1. If you needed to settle a conflict between two employees, would you
   settle on the basis of who is right and who is wrong, or would you
   decide based only on what is best for the company?

2. Suppose you are aware that two of your friends are in conflict. What would you do?

Writing Assignments

1. Write a memo to your employer reporting the process you followed in handling a conflict among your workers, the resolution of the conflict, and why the conflict was resolved as it was.
2. Suppose you are the manager of a fast-food restaurant. Write a letter to the owner of the restaurant explaining the process you followed in settling a disagreement among your employees.

It's Time to Make up Your Mind

Winston Fletcher

Sometimes it is difficult to make a decision, especially if that decision involves a conflict between your ethics and values, and your work. Maybe you choose to put off the decision. Winston Fletcher, chair of the advertising group Bozell UK, provides some suggestions for overcoming indecisiveness.

Before You Read

What are the pros and cons of the career you are considering?

Words to Know

procrastinators   people who put off doing something
prodigious   huge, enormous
propensity   tendency, inclination
shoddiness   poor or inferior quality

. . . Every day we all make hundreds of decisions with hardly a thought.   1
We decide what to have for breakfast, what to wear, which bits of the newspaper to read and which to ignore. Yet most of us feel guiltily indecisive at work, much of the time. In our hearts, we alone know what terrible procrastinators we are.

Can you improve yourself? You bet. First and foremost, in any situa-   2
tion, you must determine your objectives. The ends will almost always justify the means—but you must be absolutely clear about the ends you're aiming for. Are you willing to let your personal life suffer, or do you want to keep work and home life in balance? Are you keen to be popular or don't you give a stuff? Are you willing to be ruthless in pursuit of your ambitions or do you find ruthless behavior unethical? The more guidelines you can lay down for yourself, the faster you will decide which activities will help you achieve your goals and which won't. If you constantly hum and haw about where you are going, you'll never decide how to get there.

On any project, one of the immediate analyses you need to make is: 3
does it need to be perfect or does it need to be fast? As in cooking, excellence often takes time—time that may not be available. . . . There is never any excuse for shoddiness, but there is often a trade-off between speed

and perfection. Find out what's needed before you start or you'll end up falling out of the frying pan and into the fire. . . .

Next, evaluate the downside. What is the worst that can happen if things 4 go pear-shaped? When you're making a decision, carefully analyze the consequences of everything coming utterly unstuck. The downside will rarely be quite as disastrous as it first appears.

Then, don't delay—but don't rush. If you have a little time in hand, 5 take it: you'll find the decision keeps resurfacing in your mind, helping you to reexamine all the angles. Many of the most senior and successful business managers I have met view themselves as rather cautious decision-makers. They're not, of course. Their skill is to act as quickly as the circumstances dictate, while taking as much time as the circumstances allow. "More haste less speed" is as true in business as in life generally.

A couple more tips. If you are hesitating, ask yourself how somebody 6 you admire would tackle the problem: the head of the company, perhaps, or a previous boss you really rated. Put them in your shoes and see what they would do. It will force you to look at the problem from a different standpoint. Similarly, don't be too proud to ask for advice. Phrase your enquiry properly and it won't make you look stupid; it will make you look smart. Whereas you will indubitably look a right idiot if you make the wrong decision when your colleagues knew the right one all along. The propensity of managers to re-invent wheels is prodigious. Don't do it.

Probably the best single decision-making aid ever devised was invented 7 by the great American wit, thinker, and businessman Benjamin Franklin over 200 years ago. Franklin had made enough by the age of 42 to retire, which was probably even more difficult then than now. And he did it with the help of his "pros and cons" lists. He analyzed every decision into its pros and cons and wrote down the two lists, facing each other, on a single sheet of paper. (Today you can do it on a computer, but it's one of the few pieces of analysis I still find faster by old-fashioned pencil and paper.) The pros and cons must each be boiled down to a few words—the act of compression makes you think hard about them. And it's essential they are written down (or typed). If you try to carry them in your head, you'll get yourself into an unholy, confused, and thoroughly indecisive mess. But if you make out Ben Franklin's pros and cons lists properly, they will always help you to speedy, but considered, decisions.

Dig Deep into Your Pocket

Another system I've used and like I stole from Bob Jacoby. Bob Jacoby 8 was the dynamic supremo of the Ted Bates advertising agency for many years, and is credited with having made more money out of advertising than any other individual in history—over $100 million. (He then retired, too.) Jacoby jotted down decisions that were nagging at his mind on small pieces of paper. He put the pieces in his jacket pocket, together with other bits of paper with other difficult decisions. Whenever he had a spare moment, he would pull one of the pieces of paper from his pocket at random, and concentrate on it for a few minutes. It might not work for everyone, but it worked for him, and it has worked for me, though I still prefer Franklin's pros and cons list.

There I go again: indecisive even about the best way to become more   9
decisive. That must be why I'm never going to be head honcho at Chrysler. But maybe you could. Stop procrastinating and get on with it.

Questions About the Reading

1. What is the first task you must do to improve your decision making?
2. What is one of the immediate analyses you need to make related to a decision?
3. What should you do if you are hesitating?
4. What is the best decision-making aid, according to the writer?

Thinking Critically

1. What are the pros and cons of watching television?
2. The writer says, "The ends [objectives] will almost always justify the means—but you must be absolutely clear about the ends you're aiming for." Do you agree with this statement?

Writing Assignments

1. Assume that you are going to make some changes in a report you wrote with some classmates. In your journal, list the pros and cons of making the changes.
2. Write an informal report in memo form to the classmates in your collaborative writing group explaining the changes you want to make in their report.
3. Write a memo to your instructor reporting the progress your collaborative writing group has made on a writing assignment.

Truth and Consequences

Geanne Rosenberg

Geanne Rosenberg, an attorney, explains the possible consequences of reporting wrongdoing by fellow workers. Three human resources executives provide suggestions for handling various wrongdoing situations.

Before You Read

What would you do if you observed a coworker taking tools that belong to the company?

Words to Know

ethicist   person who studies or gives advice related to ethics
lucrative   profitable
retaliatory   pay back, punishment
scenarios   outlines, lists of possible occurrences

When attorney Colette K. Bohatch suspected a colleague at Butler & 1 Binion of overbilling a client, she told the Houston law firm's managing partner. The firm later asked her to leave, claiming client dissatisfaction with her work. In Bohatch's view, it was a retaliatory expulsion. She sued and, after a brief court battle, ended up with an award of $35,000 plus attorney's fees, small potatoes compared with the lucrative law partnership she lost.

Douglas D. Keeth also reported fraudulent billing practices at his com- 2 pany, defense contractor United Technologies Corp., where he was a division vice president of finance. He was awarded $22.5 million by the U.S. government and had the option of keeping his high-level position.

The consequences of revealing workplace wrongdoing are rarely so 3 extreme. But, as both of these cases show, choosing to blow the whistle on your employees or coworkers can create all kinds of legal, ethical, and career complications. It's never an easy decision, whether the situation is a public threat (say your employer is polluting) or more personal in nature (a colleague is sexually harassing someone or drinking on the job).

Unethical workplace conduct is surprisingly widespread. In a recent survey on business ethics by the Society for Human Resource Manage- 4 ment and the Ethics Resource Center, 54 percent of human resources professionals polled said they had observed employees running afoul of the law or of workplace standards. What did they see? Forty-five percent caught workers lying to supervisors, 36 percent observed on-the-job abuse of drugs or alcohol, and 36 percent witnessed lies in reports or the falsifying of records.

Here are five common workplace scenarios that might cause you to search your soul about whether or not to go public with potentially damaging charges. Read them carefully and think about what you'd do in each situation. Then look at what our panel of experts—a lawyer, an HR executive, and a business ethicist—advises. As you'll see from their responses, the issues are never clear-cut. One thing they all agree on: If you ever need to contact outside authorities about a workplace problem, a good place to start is your local U.S. attorney's office. To help protect your job, be sure to keep a diary of events related to the problem.

- **You believe your company is overcharging or otherwise defrauding a customer or client.**

Elletta Sangrey Callahan, a professor of law and public policy at Syracuse University's School of Management: As Keeth's case shows, if the client being overbilled is the U.S. government, you're in luck. You can report the fraud under the False Claims Act. The Justice Department will keep your complaint secret, and if the government decides to prosecute, you get a percentage of any recovery. If not, you can pursue the case on your own, as did Henry Boisvert, a former employee of defense contractor FMC Corp. Boisvert sued FMC, claiming its Bradley Fighting Vehicle failed to meet U.S. Army requirements. A jury agreed, and Boisvert stands to gain up to $100 million.

If Uncle Sam is not the client being defrauded, your legal options are more limited. Before taking any action, consult an attorney who is an expert in employment law.

Michael R. Losey, president and CEO of the Society for Human Resource Management: Take action inside the company, but avoid confronting the individuals you believe are involved. Instead, keep going up the corporate ladder until you find a manager who seems to be above the fray.

Edward Petry, executive director of the Ethics Officer Association in Belmont, Massachusetts: Reporting such a crime can be scary because you risk retaliation from management, as well as from coworkers who may see you as a traitor. If you can't go to your supervisor because he or she may be involved with the problem, discuss it with your company's corporate ethics or human resources officer.

- **With all of the headlines generated by sexual harassment cases lately, you'd think employees wouldn't dare break the law. But it's happening right under your company's nose.**

Callahan: Report your suspicions to the local office of the Equal Em- 10 ployment Opportunity Commission (call 800-669-4000). Although the EEOC is often backlogged and may not have the resources to pursue anonymous complaints, you should be able to get advice. A corporate ombudsman or human resources executive is another avenue, particularly if the office culture supports communication about sexual harassment.

Losey: Don't intervene without sufficient justification. If you suspect 11 that an incident has taken place, one approach is to ask the victim if there's anything you can do to help. If you're sure that harassment is occurring, report it to company officials.

Petry: Report any suspected sexual harassment immediately. Given the 12 legal environment, the company is at great risk if the situation is not addressed.

- **You discover that your company, or one of its divisions, products, or processes, presents a physical danger to workers or to the public.**

Callahan: Your company is probably violating some federal law, such 13 as the Occupational Safety and Health Act. Document the suspected wrongdoing carefully. Then you may want to call a lawyer. If your goal is to quickly halt the danger or misconduct, first report the incident to a company official.

Losey: Tell someone at the company. But if the situation is so serious 14 that it can't be halted from within, report it to outside officials, such as OSHA, the Environmental Protection Agency, or state and local agencies.

Petry: If the company has an internal reporting system, bypass it only 15 under extraordinary circumstances. It seems to be in everybody's interest for organizations to be responsible.

- **An employee is padding overtime statements, taking home some of the company's inventory, or stealing equipment.**

Callahan: If you have no place to turn within the company, go to your 16 local law enforcement agency. Whether you decide to report it internally or to the police, the company is unlikely to retaliate, because you're acting in its best interests.

Losey: I am continually amazed by how many people steal. When you 17 know about it or have reason to believe it's occurring, tell a company official.

Petry: Don't be hasty. No one wants to create an environment where 18 employees are blowing a whistle on coworkers for taking paper clips. A balance needs to be maintained. The danger here is creating a Big Brother atmosphere.

- **You smell alcohol on a coworker's breath and notice his work hasn't been up to standard lately.**

Callahan: Report the behavior to a higher-up, the company ombuds- 19 man, or the employee hotline. The person's drinking could put other people at risk. If criminal law is being violated—say the employee is driving drunk—local law enforcement agencies are another possible channel.

Losey: If a peer is impaired and you think it presents a health or safety 20 issue, the first thing to do is say, "Joe, I detect the alcohol." Confront the coworker and demand a promise that he will seek help. If the problem continues, go to a human resources professional who can recommend an employee assistance program.

Petry: Depending on the job, safety issues may be involved. The em- 21 ployee may also have a personal problem. It's important to address both. You may want to talk with the person one-on-one first. But if it's a pattern, then the organization has a right to know. You should bring it to the attention of the employee's immediate supervisor or the ethics officer, if your company has one.

Questions About the Reading

1. What happened to Colette K. Bohatch after she reported that a colleague overbilled a client?
2. What happened to Douglas D. Keeth after he reported fraudulent billing by his company?
3. What percentage of human resource professionals polled observed workers breaking the law or workplace standards?
4. Of the human resource professionals, what percentages caught workers lying, abusing drugs or alcohol on the job, or lying in reports or records?

Thinking Critically

1. What would you do if you discovered that an administrator of your school had filed a false academic record?
2. What would you do if you observed a coworker copying confidential company records and taking them home?

Writing Assignments

1. In your journal, list the pros and cons of reporting drug use by persons in your workplace.

2. Write a memo to your supervisor asking for a meeting to discuss a workplace problem.
3. Working with classmates, combine your journal pros-and-cons lists of reporting drug use by persons in the workplace and discuss possible courses of action. Write an informal report explaining the action the group decides to take and the pros and cons of the action. Write a letter addressed to the director of human resources of your company, Martin Electric, Inc., to transmit the report.

6

Discrimination and Harassment

IN SPITE OF laws prohibiting discrimination and harassment in the workplace based on gender, race, disability, or sexual orientation, discrimination and harassment may still occur. In "Women and Physics," K. C. Cole, a physicist, describes her experiences as a woman among her predominantly male colleagues and explains why few women choose to follow careers in the sciences.

Andrew Sullivan, in "Do We Need These Laws?" questions the need for laws protecting gays and lesbians in employment and suggests the need for equal rights laws protecting marriage and military service. Elizabeth Birch disagrees in "Earth to Andrew," citing examples of persons fired from their jobs when their sexual orientation became known.

In "Why Black Men Have Lost Ground," Peter Passell discusses the decline in wages and employment of black men over the past twenty years. Mary Ann Farrell, in "Know Your Rights—and Go for the Job" tells us that although the disabled have a harder time finding employment, they will be more successful if they know their rights.

Anne Fisher addresses the sexual harassment problem in "After All This Time, Why Don't People Know What Sexual Harassment Means?" She discusses the confusion over the definition of *sexual harassment* and *hostile environment* and provides some clarification of the definitions of the terms.

Pie Charts, Bar Charts, and Line Graphs

In this chapter you will be asked to develop a pie chart, bar chart, and line graph. These visual displays of information are used to simplify, clarify, show relationships, and condense statistical information in reports and other communications. Visual displays also make the statistics more interesting to the reader.

A pie chart compares one element or piece of information to the total information. The information is expressed in percentages. For example, the pie chart below compares the percentage of games won (60) and lost (40) by a baseball team.

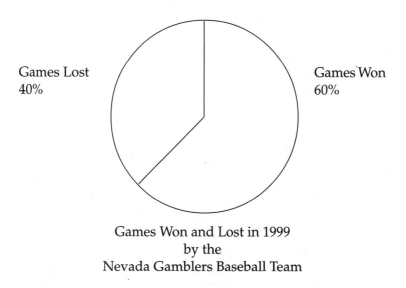

Games Lost
40%

Games Won
60%

Games Won and Lost in 1999
by the
Nevada Gamblers Baseball Team

The same information can be displayed in a bar chart by horizontal bars.

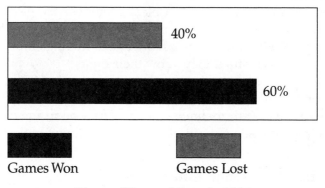

40%

60%

Games Won   Games Lost

Games Won and Lost in 1999
by the
Nevada Gamblers Baseball Team

The same information can be displayed in vertical bars.

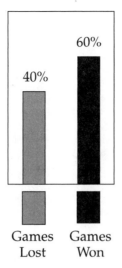

Games Won and Lost in 1999 by the Nevada Gamblers Baseball Team

A line graph is used to show trends, such as the decline in unemployment; correlations, such as the decline in unemployment and the decline in the welfare roles; or changes over time, such as the price of a stock over the years, as in the example below. Notice that the vertical axis (left side of the graph) identifies the price of the stock, from the low to the high price, and the horizontal axis identifies the time period from the earliest to the latest period.

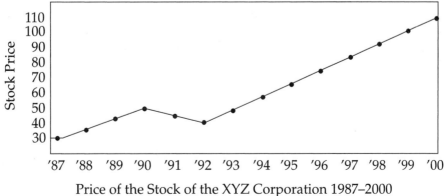

Price of the Stock of the XYZ Corporation 1987–2000

A line graph can also be used to show correlations between or among factors. The following line graph shows the correlation between the stocks of the ABC and XYZ corporations.

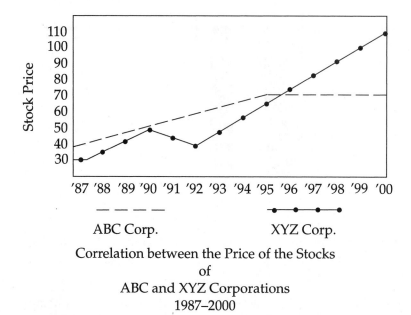

Correlation between the Price of the Stocks
of
ABC and XYZ Corporations
1987–2000

Notice that even though the information in each visual display is clear, a written explanation of the information is still included with each chart or graph.

You will probably be able to find a program on your computer for creating visual displays. Such programs make it possible to create professional-looking graphics for your reports and other communications.

Women and Physics

K. C. Cole

K. C. Cole, a physicist, discusses her experiences as a woman in what continues to be a man's field. She maintains that women are discouraged, in their early childhood treatment, from entering the scientific fields. K. C. Cole has written on women and science for the Washington Post, New York Times, New Yorker, *and other publications and is also the author of several books related to physics.*

Before You Read

Do you think women avoid the sciences because they lack the same abilities as men or because they are discouraged by the way they are raised and treated in school?

Words to Know

august famous
calculus mathematical method of analysis
comportment behavior
consequences results
injurious harmful
phenomenon unusual occurrence
physics science of matter and energy and their interactions

I know few other women who do what I do. What I do is write about 1 science, mainly physics. And to do that, I spend a lot of time reading about science, talking to scientists and struggling to understand physics. In fact, most of the women (and men) I know think me quite queer for actually liking physics. "How can you write about that stuff?" they ask, always somewhat askance. "I could never understand that in a million years." Or more simply, "I hate science."

I didn't realize what an odd creature a woman interested in physics 2 was until a few years ago when a science magazine sent me to Johns Hopkins University in Baltimore for a conference on an electrical phenomenon known as the Hall effect. We sat in a huge lecture hall and listened as physicists talked about things engineers didn't understand, and engineers talked about things physicists didn't understand. What I didn't understand was why, out of several hundred young students of physics and engineering in the room, less than a handful were women.

Some time later, I found myself at the California Institute of Technol-   3
ogy reporting on the search for the origins of the universe. I interviewed
physicist after physicist, man after man. I asked one young administrator
why none of the physicists were women. And he answered: "I don't know,
but I suppose it must be something innate. My 7-year-old daughter doesn't
seem to be much interested in science."

It was with that experience fresh in my mind that I attended a confer-   4
ence in Cambridge, Massachusetts, on science literacy, or rather the wor-
risome lack of it in this country today. We three women—a science teacher,
a young chemist, and myself—sat surrounded by a company of august
men. The chemist, I think, first tentatively raised the issue of science illit-
eracy in women. It seemed like an obvious point. After all, everyone had
agreed over and over again that scientific knowledge these days was a
key factor in economic power. But as soon as she made the point, it became clear that we women had committed a grievous social error. Our
genders were suddenly showing; we had interrupted the serious talk with
a subject unforgivably silly.

For the first time, I stopped being puzzled about why there weren't   5
any women in science and began to be angry. Because if science is a search
for answers to fundamental questions then it hardly seems frivolous to
find out why women are excluded. Never mind the economic consequences.

A lot of the reasons why women are excluded are spelled out by the   6
Massachusetts Institute of Technology experimental physicist Vera
Kistiakowsky in a recent article in *Physics Today* called "Women in Physics: Unnecessary, Injurious and Out of Place?" The title was taken from a
19th century essay written in opposition to the appointment of a female
mathematician to a professorship at the University of Stockholm. "As
decidedly as two and two make four," a woman in mathematics is a "mon-
strosity," concluded the writer of the essay.

Dr. Kistiakowsky went on to discuss the factors that make women in   7
science today, if not monstrosities, at least oddities. Contrary to much
popular opinion, one of those is *not* an innate difference in the scientific
ability of boys and girls. But early conditioning does play a stubborn and
subtle role. A recent Nova program, "The Pinks and the Blues," documented how girls and boys are treated differently from birth—the boys
always encouraged in more physical kinds of play, more active explora-
tions of their environments. Sheila Tobias, in her book, *Math Anxiety*,
showed how the games boys play help them to develop an intuitive understanding of speed, motion, and mass. The main sorting out of the girls
from the boys in science seems to happen in junior high school. As a friend
who teaches in a science museum said, "By the time we get to electricity,
the boys already have had some experience with it. But it's unfamiliar to

the girls." Science books draw on boys' experiences. "The examples are all about throwing a baseball at such and such a speed," said my step-daughter, who barely escaped being a science drop-out.

The most obvious reason there are not many more women in science is 8 that women are discriminated against as a class, in promotions, salaries, and hirings, a conclusion reached by a recent analysis by the National Academy of Sciences.

Finally, said Dr. Kistiakowsky, women are simply made to feel out of 9 place in science. Her conclusion was supported by a Ford Foundation study by Lynn H. Fox on the problems of women in mathematics. When students were asked to choose among six reasons accounting for girls' lack of interest in math, the girls rated this statement second: "Men do not want girls in the mathematical occupations."

A friend of mine remembers winning a Bronxwide mathematics com- 10 petition in the second grade. Her friends—both boys and girls—warned her that she shouldn't be good at math: "You'll never find a boy who likes you." My friend continued nevertheless to excel in math and sci-ence, won many awards during her years at the Bronx High School of Science, and then earned a full scholarship to Harvard. After one year of Harvard science, she decided to major in English.

When I asked her why, she mentioned what she called the "macho 11 mores" of science. "It would have been O.K. if I'd had someone to talk to," she said. "But the rules of comportment were such that you never admitted you didn't understand. I later realized that even the boys didn't get everything clearly right away. You had to stick with it until it had time to sink in. But for the boys, there was a payoff in suffering through the hard times, and a kind of punishment—a shame—if they didn't. For the girls it was O.K. not to get it, and the only payoff for sticking it out was that you'd be considered a freak."

Science is undeniably hard. Often, it can seem quite boring. It is unfor- 12 tunately too often presented as laws to be memorized instead of myster-ies to be explored. It is too often kept a secret that science, like art, takes a well developed esthetic sense. Women aren't the only ones who say, "I hate science." That's why everyone who goes into science needs a little help from friends. For the past ten years, I have been getting more than a little help from a friend who is a physicist. But my stepdaughter—who earned the highest grades ever recorded in her California high school on the math Scholastic Aptitude Test—flunked calculus in her first year at Harvard. When my friend the physicist heard about it, he said, "Harvard should be ashamed of itself."

What he meant was that she needed that little extra encouragement 13 that makes all the difference. Instead, she got that little extra discourage-ment that makes all the difference. "In the first place all the math teachers are men," she explained. "In the second place, when I met a boy I liked and told him I was taking chemistry, he immediately said: 'Oh, you're one of those science types.' In the third place, it's just a kind of social thing. The math clubs are full of boys and you don't feel comfortable joining."

In other words, she was made to feel unnecessary, and out of place.   14

A few months ago, I accompanied a male colleague from the science   15 museum where I sometimes work to a lunch of the history of science faculty at the University of California. I was the only woman there, and my presence for the most part was obviously and rudely ignored. I was so surprised and hurt by this that I made an extra effort to speak knowledgeably and well. At the end of the lunch, one of the professors turned to me in all seriousness and said: "Well, K. C., what do the women think of Carl Sagan?" I replied that I had no idea what "the women" thought about anything. But now I know what I should have said: I should have told him that his comment was unnecessary, injurious and out of place.

Questions About the Reading

1. What is the main idea of the essay?
2. Why does the writer think women do not enter the scientific fields?
3. What was the writer's answer to the male colleague's question at the lunch at the University of California? What does the writer think she should have said to her male colleague (paragraph 15)?

Thinking Critically

1. Would you prefer to have a woman or a man as your doctor? Why?
2. Would you vote for a woman for president of the United States? Why?

Writing Assignments

1. Working with classmates, discover the number of women and the number of men who were teaching in your school in 1995 and the number of each gender teaching in the current year. Develop a line graph showing your findings.
2. Using the same information that you collected for question 1, develop a bar chart.
3. Create a pie chart showing the percentages of women and men in the current House of Representatives of the United States Congress.

Do We Need These Laws?

Andrew Sullivan

Andrew Sullivan, author of Virtually Normal: An Argument About Homosexuality *and* Love Undetectable, *maintains that getting and keeping jobs is not the most pressing issue that homosexuals face. He maintains that focusing on equal rights—for example, in marriage and the military—should be the group's agenda.*

Before You Read

Do you think homosexuals are discriminated against in the workplace?

Words to Know

bigotry   prejudice, intolerance
irreparably   beyond repair, unchangeable
minuscule   tiny, very small
nexus   group connection or bond

Before I make myself irreparably unpopular, I might as well start with 1 a concession. Almost all the arguments the fundamentalist right uses against gay "special rights" are phony ones. If there's legal protection for blacks, whites, Jews, Latinos, women, the disabled, and now men in the workplace, then it's hard to see why homosexuals should be excluded.

It's also true that such laws would ban discrimination against straights 2 as well as gays, and so they target no single group for "special" protection. Nevertheless, there's a reason the special rights rhetoric works, and that is because it contains a germ of truth. However evenhanded antidiscrimination laws are in principle, in practice they're designed to protect the oppressed. So while the laws pretend to ban discrimination on the neutral grounds of sex, race, ethnicity, or disability, they really exist to protect women, blacks, Latinos, the disabled, and so on. They are laws that create a class of victims and a battery of lawyers and lobbyists to protect them.

The real question, then, is this: Are gay people generally victims in 3 employment? Have we historically been systematically barred from jobs in the same way that, say, women, blacks, and the disabled have? And is a remedy therefore necessary? My own view is that, while there are some particular cases of discrimination against homosexuals, for the most part getting and keeping jobs is hardly the most pressing issue we face. Aided by our talents, by the ability of each generation to avoid handing on poverty to the next, and by the two-edged weapon of the closet, we have, by and large, avoided becoming economic victims. Even in those states where job-protection laws have been enacted, sexual orientation cases have made up a minuscule proportion of the whole caseload.

Most people—gay and straight—know this to be true; and so they sense   4
that the push for gay employment rights is unconvincing and whiny. I think they're right. The truth is, most gay people are not victims, at least not in the economic sense. We may not be much richer than most Americans, but there's little evidence that we are much poorer. Despite intense psychological, social, and cultural hostility, we have managed to fare pretty well economically in the past few generations. Instead of continually whining that we need job protection, we should be touting our economic achievements, defending the free market that makes them possible, investing our resources in our churches and charities and social institutions, and politically focusing on the areas where we clearly are discriminated against by our own government.

The problems of gay and lesbian Americans are not, after all, system-   5
atic exclusion from employment. They are (to name a few off the top of my head): a recourse to the closet, a lack of self-esteem, an inability to form lasting relationships, the threat of another epidemic, exclusion from our own churches, and our own government's denial of basic rights, such as marriage, immigration, and military service. In this sense, employment discrimination is a red herring.

National gay rights groups love it because they are part of the lobby-   6
ist-lawyer nexus that will gain from it and because their polls tell them it's the least objectionable of our aims. But anyone could tell them it's the least objectionable because it's the least relevant.

Of course, we're told that until we're protected from discrimination in   7
employment, we'll never be able to come out of the closet and effect the deeper changes we all want. But this is more victim-mongering. Who says gay people can't risk something for their own integrity? Who says a civil rights revolution can only occur when every single protection is already in place? If African-Americans in the 1960s had waited for such a moment, there would still be segregation in Alabama.

Our national leaders should spend less time making excuses for us   8
and more time challenging us to risk our own lives and, yes, if necessary, jobs to come out and make a difference for the next generation. An "equal rights" rather than "special rights" agenda would focus on those areas in which gay people really are discriminated against. After all, have you heard any fundamentalist "special rights" rhetoric in the marriage debate? Or in the military battle? Not a squeak. What you hear instead is a

revealing mumble of bigotry in opposition. And in these areas of clear government discrimination, we stand on firm, moral ground instead of the muddy bog of interest-group politics. In an equal-rights politics, we reverse the self-defeating logic of victim culture. We are proud and proactive instead of defensive and cowed. And we stop framing a movement around the tired 1970s mantra of "what we want" and start building one around the 1990s vision of "who we actually want to be."

Questions About the Reading

1. Who are the equal rights laws designed to protect?
2. Does the writer think homosexuals are economic victims? Are they richer or poorer than most Americans?
3. What does the writer say that homosexuals should be "touting"?
4. What does the writer say are the problems of gay and lesbian Americans?

Thinking Critically

1. Would legalizing marriage between homosexuals be giving them a "special right"?
2. Do you agree with the "don't ask, don't tell" policy regarding homosexuals serving in the military forces?
3. What would you do if your coworkers were discriminating against another worker?

Writing Assignments

1. Write an essay in which you explain and give examples of the difference between equal rights and special rights.
2. Working with classmates, research antidiscrimination laws and write an informal report analyzing their values and shortcomings.

Earth to Andrew

Elizabeth Birch

Elizabeth Birch, executive director of Human Rights Campaign, disagrees strongly with Andrew Sullivan. She argues that discrimination against homosexuals in the workplace is a serious problem and that there is a need for antidiscrimination laws to protect them.

Before You Read

Do you agree with Andrew Sullivan or with Elizabeth Birch?

Words to Know

cavalier   arrogant, haughty
disseminated   distributed, handed out
distraught   upset, concerned
ostensibly   supposedly

Each morning when the alarm clock rings, thousands of lesbian and   1
gay Americans wake up with knots in their stomachs. From line workers to executives, from short-order cooks to engineers, they fear this may be the day when their livelihoods are ripped away from them and their families.

Like other organizations, the Human Rights Campaign receives a steady   2
stream of phone calls from distraught individuals who were fired from their jobs simply because of their sexual orientation. It is distressing to realize that in 40 states, it is perfectly legal to discriminate against gay Americans in the workplace. We also know that for every person who calls us with a horror story, there are just as many people who don't call us because they know they are not legally protected.

Based on our numerous experiences, we were amazed when Andrew   3
Sullivan questioned, in the April 14 edition of The Advocate, the need for antidiscrimination laws such as the Employment Non-Discrimination Act, which is pending federal legislation that would protect lesbians, gay men, and bisexuals from job discrimination. Perhaps even more puzzling was his questioning of whether job discrimination against lesbians and gay men was even a problem. It is possible that Sullivan has never experienced job discrimination, but we can assure him there are thousands of gay people who have.

According to a 1996 poll conducted by the ICR Survey Group for Lake 4
Research, 82% of the gay people surveyed cited a law to protect gay people
from discrimination in employment as "one of the most important issues" facing the community.

A complete disconnect in logic occurs when Sullivan denies this is a 5
problem, then turns around and says that he recognizes that gays endure
"intense psychological, social, and cultural hostility." If this hostile climate exists as he says it does, how can he believe that these hostile attitudes simply disappear when a gay person punches the time clock? Take
Mark Anderson's experience, for instance.

Anderson, who worked for a high-powered consulting firm in Califor- 6
nia, arrived home from a business trip one afternoon to confront a chill-
ing sight. His car had been stolen and returned, repainted as a police car,
covered with antigay epithets like "Rump Ranger" and "1-800-BUTT-
BOY." What really made this incident scar, however, was that it was not
street thugs who were responsible for this crime but Anderson's coworkers. To complete his nightmare, the makeover on his car was videotaped
and disseminated at his company's biennial sales meeting. Shortly after
this episode, Anderson was terminated.

Many discrimination cases are not this dramatic. A more typical case is 7
that of Sue Kirchofer, a three-year employee of a Seattle-based distribu-
tor, who had received annual raises and praise from management for her
job performance. For her annual vacation, Kirchofer went to compete in
the Gay Games. Before she left she told a few coworkers of her plans.
Two days after returning from the games, she was fired, ostensibly for
low quarterly earnings.

Incredibly, Sullivan accuses those hurt by discrimination, such as 8
Anderson and Kirchofer, and the national organizations who try to assist
them of engaging in the "self-defeating logic" of "victim-mongering."
He goes on to say, "Who says gay people can't risk something [their jobs]
for their own integrity?" HRC agrees with Sullivan that people should
"come out," and we help thousands take this difficult step each year
through our National Coming Out Project. However, it is cavalier to suggest that people who may be raising children or caring for a partner lack
integrity. When he flippantly suggests that people abort their careers, is
he thinking of the lesbian couple with average jobs who are trying to put
their children through school?

Fortunately, according to a bipartisan 1997 poll, the majority of Ameri- 9
cans recognize what Sullivan does not. The poll found that 68% of
Americans support ENDA. It is also clear that we must work toward pro-
tections based on gender identity. In 1996 ENDA was one vote short of
passage in the Senate, and it has a solid chance of passing this year. That

is, if people such as Andrew Sullivan would stop trivializing the traumatic workplace experiences that many lesbians and gay men have endured.

Questions About the Reading

1. According to the writer, is it legal to discriminate against gays in the workplace?
2. What is the antidiscrimination act that the writer says should be passed?
3. Who was responsible for painting Mark Anderson's car?
4. What percentage of Americans, according to the writer, support the Employment Non-Discrimination Act?

Thinking Critically

1. Do you think people with disabilities are discriminated against in the workplace?
2. What do you think are legitimate reasons for not employing a person?
3. What do you think are legitimate reasons for terminating a person's employment?
4. Do you think what was done to Mark Anderson could be considered harassment?

Writing Assignments

1. Write a report explaining the provisions of the Employment Non-Discrimination Act.
2. Working with classmates, write an essay explaining whether current antidiscrimination laws are adequate or whether additional laws are needed. If additional laws are needed, explain what they should address.

Why Black Men Have Lost Ground

Peter Passell

In this article, written for the New York Times *in 1991, Peter Passell considers the reasons for the decline in employment of black men over the 1973–1989 time period.*

Before You Read

Do you think black men have had a harder time finding work during the current economic period than their white counterparts have? Why or why not?

Words to Know

deteriorated declined

disproportionate unequal in relative size or amount

parallel equal in distance

Rust Belt heavy manufacturing area of the North and Midwest, characterized by steel production

spectrum range, total span

stagnating standing still

statistical regression mathematical calculation related to the value of a variable or factor

---

It is no great puzzle why young male workers have had to run so hard 1 over the last 15 years simply to stay in place. They are the first generation to compete with women workers on a nearly equal basis. More important, they are the first postwar generation to enter the labor market when labor productivity was barely growing.

The mystery is why, in spite of the triumphs of the civil rights move- 2 ment, young black men have lost ground to their white counterparts during the period.

Economists like simple explanations—especially ones that point toward 3 simple policy fixes. But in this case, argue John Bound of the University of Michigan and Richard Freeman of Harvard, simplicity is the enemy of truth.

No single cause stands out in their analysis of stagnating employment 4 opportunities for black men, published last month in a National Bureau of Economic Research working paper. Anything that could go wrong it

seems, has gone wrong, damaging the job prospects of black college graduates as well as high school dropouts.

There is no disputing that the drive for racial equality in the workplace 5
ran out of steam in the mid-1970s. Adjusted for education levels, the gap
in weekly earnings for black men and white men with less than 10 years
of work experience fell from 35 percent in 1963 to just 11 percent in 1975.
But since then, it has crept back up to 18 percent.

Young black men face parallel problems in getting jobs. In 1973 the 6
black-white gap in employment rates was 9 percentage points; by 1989 it
had widened to 15.

What happened? Many small things rather than one big thing.   7

The researchers divided black men by region (Northeast, Midwest, 8
South) and by education (college graduates, high school graduates, dropouts). All of these subgroups lost ground on wages and (with one modest
exception) on employment rates as well. But the differences in the rate of
loss are striking.

College graduates did especially badly on wages. The white-black dif- 9
ferences for college graduates widened three times faster than the gap for
high school graduates and six times faster than the gap for dropouts.
Midwestern blacks were also particularly big losers, losing far more
ground than their Southern counterparts.

The pattern is somewhat different on rates of employment. Dropouts' 10
prospects deteriorated far more rapidly than the prospects for all young
male blacks. And in contrast to Southerners and Midwesterners, young
male blacks in the Northeast actually gained a little on whites.

Using statistical regression techniques to dig deeper, the economists 11
found that blacks had the misfortune of being in the wrong places and
the wrong occupations at the wrong time. For example, relatively more
depend on minimum-wage jobs for a living. The erosion of the minimum
wage as a fraction of average wages is all that is needed to explain 17
percent of the ground lost by young male blacks. Similarly, a disproportionate number were union members. Thus as union wages fell relative
to wages in general, blacks lost more than whites—a phenomenon that
explains 5 percent of the change in the earnings gap.

Then there are the twin problems of occupation and industry. More 12
blacks wore blue collars and more worked in manufacturing. Both groups
suffered heavily in the early 1980s, when foreign competition savaged
the Rust Belt. This one-two punch accounts for 29 percent of the relative
decline in the wages of young blacks.

Slippage in employment rates is largely a problem at the unskilled end 13
of the job spectrum. And here, Mr. Bound and Mr. Freeman look to crime

and punishment for the explanation: Between 1980 and 1989 the proportion of black high school dropouts in jail or on probation has grown by one-fifth. This explains fully 71 percent of the downward trend in black dropouts at work.

These results should depress people who look to government to pro- 14 mote equality of result as well as equality of opportunity. The great forces of history that have exposed the American economy to global competition and have led to a restructuring of industry probably cannot be stopped. Even if they could, few policy makers would be inclined to reverse course solely to keep black workers out of harm's way.

By the same token, Americans already have very good reasons to end 15 the plague of urban street crime. The fact that crime leaves so many young black men effectively unemployable is not, in itself, likely to move public policy.

About the best that can be said here is that the worst is probably over. 16 The regional economic shifts that worked to the disadvantage of blacks have apparently ended. So, too, have the shifts in labor demand that made blue-collar workers such a drag on the market during the 1980s. With a little luck, future trends will prove colorblind—or even work to the advantage of racial minorities.

Questions About the Reading

1. What is the general reason the writer says is the cause of the decline in employment of all male workers over the 1970s to 1990s?
2. According to the writer, what was the impact on black employment of the decline in the minimum wage in relation to average wages?
3. What is the relation of crime and punishment to the downward trend in black employment, according to the writer?
4. What was the percentage difference between black-white male employment in 1973 and in 1989?

Thinking Critically

1. If black men and women are discriminated against in employment, what do you think they need to do to change the situation?
2. What other groups do you think employers discriminate against? Why?
3. What are the legitimate reasons an employer might have for not employing a black, Hispanic, disabled, or elderly person?

Writing Assignments

1. Using the statistics in paragraph 5, develop a line graph. Be sure to title your graph.
2. Using the most recent census figures for your town or state, develop a pie chart showing the percent of blacks, Hispanics, Asians, whites, and other races.
3. Using the census figures for the United States from 1960 through 1990, develop a line graph showing the percent of blacks, Hispanics, Asians, whites, and other races in the total population.

Know Your Rights—And Go for the Job

Mary Ann Farrell

Mary Ann Farrell, quoting Barbara Bernhart, director of Florida's Coordinating Council on the Americans with Disabilities Act, says that disabled persons will be more successful in finding work if they know their rights. Farrell also explains the provisions of the act.

Before You Read

Does everyone have certain rights when they are seeking employment? If so, what are those rights?

Words to Know

exempt   free of, not required

impairment   diminished ability, handicap

Barbara Bernhart, Florida's director of the Coordinating Council on the   1
Americans with Disabilities Act, says even though the disabled do have
more difficulty finding work, they should not give up. If they know their
legal rights and their accommodation needs, they will be more successful.

"On a job interview, for example, do not bring up a discussion of your   2
disability, even when it's visible. When you do that, you're opening the
door to eliminating one of your rights. You may not want to discuss your
disability at all; it may be very private. You don't have to. Discuss only
how you can do this job. Under the ADA, it's now illegal for the potential
employer to ask you any health question either on your application or in
an interview." An employer may, however, ask a disabled applicant about
the ability to perform specific job functions. Within limitations, he may
also ask that person how those functions can be met with that particular
disability.

Under the Americans with Disabilities Act (ADA), any public or pri-   3
vate business with a staff of 15 or more people is now required by law to
be accessible. Reasonable accommodation must be provided to the disabled. A company, however, does not have to provide that access if the
changes would cause a financial hardship. They are also exempt from
ADA when the changes would alter the business's original intent.

Let's say you are a recently graduated chef who uses a wheelchair. You   4
apply for a job at a well-known restaurant where the entire kitchen has

already been set up. For the owner to redo the kitchen completely would
be considered a hardship. Bernhart says this would be an unreasonable
accommodation, and changes would not have to be made. Still, she says,
don't give up.

"At the time of the interview, the disabled applicant has no idea about 5
the owner's financial situation. Don't assume that employer wouldn't be
willing to accommodate. He might be looking for a write-off or a loss."
Employers are allowed to take a federal tax credit to make accommodations for the disabled. That credit, she adds, can go as high as $15,000 a
year when major architectural barriers and complete renovations are involved.

Bernhart has an excellent, real-life example. A well-known Central 6
Florida surf and beach shop recently put in a whole range of disabled
accommodations to make sure all employees could get around the public
store easily. After the changes were made, she says, the owner pleasantly
discovered accessibility meant a fantastic savings of both time and money
to his company.

"Suddenly everybody could use the elevator to get things up to the 7
second floor. It was no longer a big thing to get from one place to another.
The owner could not only display his things faster, but that, of course,
meant he could sell them faster, too. Again, when you're in an interview
situation, you just never know what's going on behind the scenes. This
owner had a disabled mother, and he wanted his mom to be able to come
inside his store. He made more than the necessary changes. So don't assume—ever."

Bernhart gives another employment situation involving intent. "Let's 8
say you're a cocktail waitress who has a visual impairment and you're
applying for a job in a new town. You notice in the lounge the lights are
dim and you have trouble seeing. You didn't have that before. Could you
ask the owner to turn up the lights? No, that would probably ruin the
atmosphere the owner's worked so hard to create, would alter the nature
of the business, another unreasonable accommodation. But could you,
say, ask that employer to give you a small flashlight to help take orders?
Yes. That's reasonable accommodation."

"It doesn't always mean knocking out a whole wall to put in a heavy- 9
duty elevator," she explains. "There are stair gliders that can work, closet
elevators. Employers shouldn't immediately panic. There are a lot of products out there now and employers and disabled job seekers owe it to themselves to investigate them and know where they can be found." It is
helpful, Bernhart says, for a disabled candidate to know before the interview starts what he may need for his particular situation. Businesses think
it will cost thousands of dollars, but Bernhart has found that most accommodations cost less than $50. The actual providing of reasonable accom-

modations on the job falls upon the employer. It does not fall upon the disabled looking for work.

Bernhart says in the backs of their minds, many disabled are still afraid 10 when they go to an interview. In no way does the ADA force an employer to hire the disabled, and for all the new changes in the law, it still can come down to which applicant that employer wants to hire, which applicant he or she feels has the best qualifications. But when you know what your rights are, it's a little easier.

Questions About the Reading

1. What is Bernhart's advice about the topics that disabled persons should and should not discuss during a job interview?
2. What can an employer ask a disabled person during a job interview?
3. What are the exemptions an employer has under the Americans with Disabilities Act?
4. What are the tax credits employers can take for accommodating the disabled?

Thinking Critically

1. Suppose you are the owner of a store specializing in large, museum-quality glass and crystal items and a person who is wheelchair-bound applies for a selling job. How would you handle the situation?
2. Suppose you are building a high-rise office complex and a carpenter with an artificial leg applies for work. How would you handle the situation and comply with the Americans with Disabilities Act?

Writing Assignments

1. Write a short, informal report explaining the provisions of the Americans with Disabilities Act.
2. Write a letter to a disabled applicant denying employment and explaining why the applicant cannot be employed in your particular business.

After All This Time, Why Don't People Know What Sexual Harassment Means?

Anne Fisher

Anne Fisher tells us that, even though sexual harassment has been illegal since 1977, people still do not have a clear idea about what it is and what it is not.

Before You Read

What do you think constitutes sexual harassment in the workplace?

Words to Know

mystification   lack of understanding
plaintiffs   persons initiating a lawsuit
precedents   examples from the past
torrent   flood

Dear Readers: It's a very odd state of affairs (no pun intended): Sexual 1
harassment in the workplace has been illegal under federal law since 1977, and in the past two decades has unquestionably gotten far more ink and airplay in the media than all other personnel issues combined. Not to mention all those stern memos you keep getting from the human resources department (well, okay, the lawyers actually write them) about company policy. You would think by now that everyone would have a pretty clear idea of what sexual harassment is and is not.

Alas, you would be wrong. A letter . . . , from someone who signed 2
herself "Drained," brought forth a torrent of e-mails pretty clearly demonstrating that on this subject, lots of folks are utterly clueless. That doesn't stop anybody from filing a lawsuit, of course: The Equal Employment Opportunity Commission in Washington reports that between 1990 and 1996, formal sexual harassment complaints filed with the agency jumped 150%, to 15,342 in 1996. Says Betsy Plevan, a partner at Proskauer Rose in Manhattan and a leading defender of companies against such claims: "There is still a tremendous amount of confusion—and a few years from now, I have no doubt there still will be." Judith Vladeck, a prominent plaintiffs attorney . . . , suspects that "a lot of the confusion is deliberate. People who are against any kind of feminist advance in the workplace spread these absurd rumors, like, 'Oh, if you even tell someone you like

the blouse they're wearing, they can sue you.' It's arrant nonsense, yet people believe it."

Well. A certain degree of mystification is understandable for at least 3 three reasons. First, in trying to ward off costly and embarrassing legal actions, many companies set a far higher standard for acceptable behavior in this area than the law requires. Just look at the infamous "Seinfeld case"—you know, where Miller Brewing Co. fired Jerold Mackenzie for showing somebody a page in a dictionary; he sued to get his job back, and a jury (with, let us note, ten women on it) awarded him $26 million. "Where is the line between bad taste and outright harassment? A company can discipline an employee for behavior that does not meet the legal standard for sexual harassment," says Plevan. "Generally, just poor taste or questionable language is not enough to constitute harassment."

On this point, lawyers on both sides of the table agree. Says Vladeck: 4 "Where we get into trouble with definitions, in the public mind, is that people hear this phrase 'hostile environment harassment,' and they think it means any kind of annoying behavior—that you can sue someone because they offend you or get on your nerves. But that is not what the law says. Nor should it."

The second reason so many people are in the dark about all this is that, 5 as with attempts to define obscenity, harassment may, to some extent, be in the eye of the beholder. What is acceptable or even routine in one community, or one corporate culture, may not be at all okay somewhere else. Women on Wall Street, for instance, have long tolerated an adolescent locker-room mentality that would shock people in more, um, buttoned-down workplaces. Usually juries take this into account, so their decisions don't—and arguably shouldn't—create any uniform standard.

And third, even a close look at a fast-growing body of court prece- 6 dents does not do much to clear things up. On the one hand, you have the Supreme Court's 1993 landmark decision in *Harris* v. *Forklift Systems*, which held that an intimidating or abusive environment (Harris' boss used to make her fish coins out of his pants pockets and proposed negotiating her raise at a nearby Holiday Inn) is indeed actionable, even if it does not "seriously affect [an employee's] psychological well-being."

On the other hand, just this past summer you have *Robinson* v. *City of* 7 *Pittsburgh*. In this case, the U.S. Court of Appeals for the Third Circuit decided that plaintiffs have no case unless they can show that sexual harassment "affected a tangible condition of employment"—that is, unless plaintiffs have been fired, suspended, or denied a promotion because they wouldn't play the game. Between these two extremes are lots of other cases, and resulting legal standards, that (trust me) you don't even want to hear about.

So let's say that all you want is to stay out of trouble here. Believe it or   8
not, it's easy. Here's what you can do: Compliment people on their ward-
robes or hair or whatever the heck you like. Ask people out if you want
to. (Even more than once is okay.) Don't bother pretending you haven't
noticed that, yes, people do bring their hormones to work with them.

Here's what you can't do: Threaten anybody with any adverse conse-   9
quences if they choose not to canoodle with you. Go out of your way to
make people feel like mindless objects who exist for your amusement
and for no other purpose. Embarrass people by pointing up their sexual
features to others. Make such a pest of yourself that it is impossible for
anyone to do her (or his) best work in the job that she (or he) is being paid
to do.

In short, conduct yourself like a decent human being. "When we do   10
sexual harassment training workshops in companies, we ask people to
look at different kinds of insensitive or abusive behavior and ask themselves, Is this appropriate for the workplace?" says Betsy Plevan. "Is this
something you would want to read about yourself in the *Wall Street Journal*? Would you want your mother to hear about it? In other words, Are
you proud of this?" Adds Vladeck: "Even the most thickheaded people
will suddenly 'get it' if you ask them, Would you like someone to treat
your daughter this way?" Enough said.

Questions About the Reading

1. According to the writer, what are the three reasons why people are
   mystified about what sexual harassment means?
2. What can people do that is not considered sexual harassment?
3. What are some of the things that the writer says could be considered
   sexual harassment?
4. What is the question Vladeck says to ask oneself when deciding
   whether an action would be considered sexual harassment?

Thinking Critically

1. Would you consider it sexual harassment if a coworker asked you to
   go out to dinner? Would it matter whether the coworker was a man or
   a woman?
2. Would you consider it harassment or discrimination if a person of a
   different race and gender got a promotion that you felt you had earned?
   How would you handle the situation?

Writing Assignments

1. Using the Equal Employment Opportunity Commission statistics in paragraph 2, calculate the number of formal sexual harassment complaints filed in 1990. Develop a line graph showing the number in 1990 and in 1996.
2. Write a memo to your employer reporting an action that you consider to be harassment.

7

Technology and
the Workplace

IF YOU ARE not already computer literate, be prepared: you will need to be. Communication in your workplace may be primarily by e-mail. You may need to use the Internet, which is valuable—even essential in most companies—not just for e-mail within your company but also for business-to-business communications such as ordering materials, getting information, confirming shipments, contacting customers, and for research.

In an article from *USA Today* magazine, "The Ins and Outs of E-Mail," the writer provides some tips for writing e-mail messages. For all its value, however, is it possible to become overly attached to the Internet? Kimberly S. Young warns against Internet addiction in "Caught in the Net." Indeed, Internet addiction may not be limited to a person's use of the Internet at home. Many companies have begun to keep track of their employees' personal use of the Internet on the job, as Deborah Branscum points out in "bigbrother@the.office.com."

Technology has also presented options for where and when workers can meet their employment responsibilities. With the technology now available, more employees are working from home. Edward C. Baig discusses the advantages and disadvantages of telecommuting to both company and employee in "Saying Adios to the Office."

E-mail

In this chapter, you will write several e-mail messages as well as reports and essays based on information obtained through the Internet. An e-mail to a friend or family member will of course be less formal than one to a business associate. In either case, it is important to be cautious about what you say and to remember that e-mail can be forwarded and archived, and that it might be read by someone other than the person to whom it is addressed. The following is an example of an e-mail message to a friend. Notice that the language is informal, but the subject and purpose of the message are clear.

From: Martin Jones / mj201@aol.com
To: bgardner@compuserve.com
Date: Sunday, August 08, 1999 4:31 P.M.
Subject: Pop Art Exhibit

I want to see the Pop Art exhibit that opens at the Museum of Art on February 19. Would you be able to go that day or a day soon after February 19?

The following example of a business e-mail is more formal in language. It provides specific information about what the sender wants to do, when he wants to do it, how much time will be involved, and what he wants to know.

From: James Martin / jm181@aol.com
To: William Barth / wb245@aol.com
Cc: Sandra West / sw412@aol.com
Date: Sunday, August 08, 1999 4:52 P.M.
Subject: Agenda Item

I have completed the advertising plan for the management seminar and would like to present it to the board on March 10, at the 9:00 A.M. meeting you have scheduled. I estimate I will need approximately a half hour to present the plan. Please let me know if this can be arranged.

Internet Research

You can find almost anything through the Internet—from job availability to the price of an airplane ticket. But it is not easy or quick to find the information you want until you have learned how to target your searches.

If you are researching a subject, it is helpful to think of the Internet as a collection of the resources of hundreds and hundreds of libraries. As you would in a library, you can start with the subject. Suppose, for example, that you are looking for a job. You can start with "jobs available" as the subject of your search. This keyword search brings up a list of Web sites, usually ten at a time. If you do not find a site description that fits your needs, you can go to the next ten sites.

Suppose "AmerUSJobs" is one of the sites listed. Clicking on that site brings up the following page.

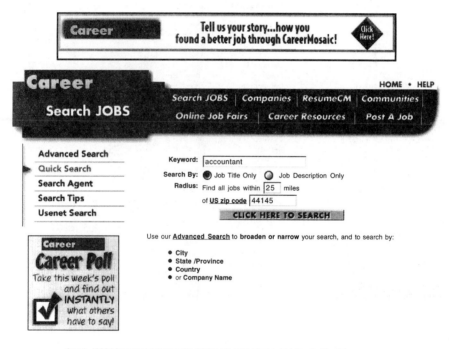

By filling in "accountant" as the job you are looking for and asking to find all jobs within 25 miles of zip code 44145, the following list of available jobs is displayed.

Career | Post your resume to ResumeCM! | Click Here!

Career

Search Jobs Results

15-JUL-00	Administrative Assistant (Accounting)	Cleveland, OH	
15-JUL-00	Accountant - Staff	CLEVELAND, OH	Accountemps
15-JUL-00	Accounting Clerk	CLEVELAND, OH	Accountemps
15-JUL-00	Accounting Clerk	CLEVELAND, OH	Accountemps
15-JUL-00	Accountant (Entry Level)	Elyria, Oh	Accountemps
15-JUL-00	Awesome accountant position with real estate background	BEACHWOOD, OH	Accountemps
15-JUL-00	Accounting Clerk	CLEVELAND, OH	Accountemps
14-JUL-00	ACCOUNTANT	Cleveland, OH	Robert Half
14-JUL-00	PLANT ACCOUNTANT	Cleveland, OH	Robert Half
14-JUL-00	SENIOR ACCOUNTANT	Cleveland, OH	Robert Half
14-JUL-00	SENIOR ACCOUNTANT	Cleveland, OH	Robert Half
14-JUL-00	SENIOR TAX ACCOUNTANT	Cleveland, OH	Robert Half
14-JUL-00	STAFF ACCOUNTANT	Cleveland, OH	Robert Half
14-JUL-00	SENIOR ACCOUNTANT	Cleveland, OH	Robert Half
14-JUL-00	SENIOR ACCOUNTANT	Cleveland, OH	Robert Half
14-JUL-00	FIXED ASSET ACCOUNTANT	Cleveland, OH	Robert Half
14-JUL-00	SENIOR ACCOUNTANT	Cleveland, OH	Robert Half
14-JUL-00	ACCOUNTING MANAGER	Cleveland, OH	Robert Half
14-JUL-00	ACCOUNTANT	Cleveland, OH	Robert Half
14-JUL-00	Staff Accountant	Cleveland, OH	Robert Half
14-JUL-00	Accounting Clerk	CLEVELAND, OH	Accountemps
14-JUL-00	STAFF ACCOUNTANT	Cleveland, OH	Robert Half
14-JUL-00	SENIOR COST ACCOUNTANT	Cleveland, OH	Robert Half
14-JUL-00	STAFF ACCOUNTANT	Cleveland, OH	Robert Half
14-JUL-00	ACCOUNTING MANAGER	Cleveland, OH	Robert Half
14-JUL-00	SENIOR ACCOUNTANT	Cleveland, OH	Robert Half
14-JUL-00	ACCOUNTING SUPERVISOR	Cleveland, OH	Robert Half
13-JUL-00	Tax Accountants	Cleveland, OH, OH	Resources Connection
13-JUL-00	Payroll Accounting Manager	Cleveland, OH, OH	Resources Connection
13-JUL-00	Accounting/Finance Professionals w/ IPO	Cleveland, OH, OH	Resources Connection
07-JUL-00	Accountant IV/Internal Auditor	Cleveland, OH	City of Cleveland
06-JUL-00	Accounting Manager	Cleveland, OH	New Times, Inc.
05-JUL-00	Real Estate Accountants	Cleveland, OH, OH	Resources Connection
04-JUL-00	Club Accountant in Development	Cleveland, OH	ClubCorp
03-JUL-00	Internal Revenue Agent (Accountant) GS-512-5/7/9	nationwide, --	Internal Revenue Service - IRS
03-JUL-00	SENIOR ACCOUNTANT	Middleburg Heights, OH	RTM Restaurant Group
01-JUL-00	Cost Accountant	Independence, OH	Kforce.com
01-JUL-00	Corporate Accounting Manager	Cleveland, OH	Kforce.com

http://jobs.careermosaic.com/j2/owa/srch.jl?hf=
JOBS.NEW3&hf2=JOBS.NEW3a&cn=USA&mm=75&ti=

01-JUL-00	Recruiter, Finance/Accounting	Cleveland, OH	Kforce.com
01-JUL-00	STAFF ACCOUNTANT	Cleveland, OH	Kforce.com
01-JUL-00	Sr. Cost Accountant	Cleveland, OH	Kforce.com
01-JUL-00	Senior Tax Accountant	Cleveland, OH	Kforce.com
01-JUL-00	Senior Tax Accountant	Cleveland, OH	Kforce.com
01-JUL-00	Senior Accountant	Cleveland, OH	Kforce.com
01-JUL-00	GENERAL ACCOUNTANT	Cleveland, OH	Kforce.com
01-JUL-00	General Accountant	Cleveland, OH	Kforce.com
01-JUL-00	MANAGER OF ACCOUNTING & AUDIT	Cleveland, OH	Kforce.com
23-JUN-00	Staff Accountant	Cleveland, OH	Volt Services Group

Too many jobs? Use the search form below to revise your search. You can narrow your search by using more keywords, or by narrowing your "Search Radius."

Would you like to see more jobs? Using the form below, try widening your "Search Radius" or using less keywords. You can also use partial words such as "manag" if you are looking for "management" jobs or a "General Manager" position.

The Internet was used as a research tool to locate many of the readings included in this text. Through a local library and a home connection, an information base called InfoTrac was accessed. Under InfoTrac, various sources, such as magazines, newspapers, and books, were available. Magazines and newspapers were searched using the chapter subjects in this text. From the library, copies of the various articles selected were e-mailed to the computer at home, accessed on the home computer, and then printed for further consideration and possible use. "The Ins and Outs of E-mail" is an example of a reading found through InfoTrac by searching first with the keyword "technology" and then narrowing the search to "e-mail."

Using the Internet takes patience, especially at first when you are working through ad-cluttered Web pages. However, it is a skill you will undoubtedly need and will find helpful and convenient both personally and in your future work.

The Ins and Outs of E-mail

USA Today *Magazine*

Keep the message short, keep it clear, and remember that other people can read your message. That is the advice offered by USA Today *magazine on using e-mail.*

Before You Read

Have you written a letter to a friend lately?

Words to Know

brevity shortness, conciseness
constrained limited
cumbersome burdensome
inherently basically
transcend overcome

Electronic mail has captivated people around the world, but experts 1
say it often is abused, misused, or misunderstood. This medium, which almost was nonexistent 10 years ago, now pervades the home and office. The rules for intelligently using e-mail bear about as much resemblance to old-fashioned mail as the telephone did to the Pony Express.

"We're all just learning in this area, and frankly we're discovering what 2
works as we go along," maintains Vicki Collins, an assistant professor of English and director of the Writing Intensive Curriculum at Oregon State University, Corvallis. "This is a brand new way of communicating. The biggest single mistake most people make when using e-mail is not to consider who may be reading the mail and what is appropriate for that person. Often, the communication is seen as inherently informal, since people frequently e-mail casual notes to friends. But communicating with professional colleagues, professors, or prospective employers requires more clarity and care."

Further complicating the situation is the fact that the convenience of 3
editing, saving, and forwarding e-mail opens a can of worms that never existed before. You don't know who might be getting the message you send, or in what altered form. "In the old days, it was rare for someone to take a written letter, photocopy it, then address and mail the correspondence to some third party. That's no longer the case. With the convenience

of electronic forwarding, your message may now be sent to one or dozens of people who you never intended to see it. Keep that in mind." Collins offers other key tips:

- Keep it brief. With e-mail, there is an underlying assumption of brevity. People expect messages to be short and to the point and get irritated when they are not.
- Understand the medium. For instance, only the first 24 lines of a message show on the average computer screen. Take advantage of that by confining your message to that space if possible and make your most important points in the first few lines. Think twice about attaching extra files or using them for your message because they get garbled in electronic translation far more often than the body of an e-mail message.
- Don't get lost. Many people get dozens of e-mail messages a day, which easily are confused or ignored if the subject line says something vague like "new idea." Be more specific and descriptive with the subject line so your message can be identified easily, relocated, and doesn't get lost in the shuffle.
- Cut to the chase. When responding to other people's e-mail, don't necessarily send them back a copy of their entire message. That's cumbersome. Yet, don't exclude their message completely or they may have forgotten why they contacted you. The best plan is to copy the pertinent section of their message in your reply so they know exactly what you are responding to.
- Be orderly. Unlike other forms of printed information that allow people to flip around and focus their attention on what interests them most, e-mail usually is read sequentially. Keep that in mind and try hard to get the most important information up front.
- Assume it's public. Privacy is a big concern with the Internet and e-mail, and the best advice before you transmit something is to assume almost anyone can see it. Your message may be forwarded to someone you did not intend it for or archived electronically without your knowledge and later come back to haunt you.
- Think first; talk later. Before you leap into the discussion in a chat room or other public forum such as an online debate, make sure your comments are appropriate for the group discussion. Consider "lurking" for a while and monitoring what other people are saying before you jump in.
- Put your best foot forward. It is okay to be informal or casual if you are sure of your audience or situation. When in doubt, use complete sentences and good grammar, punctuation, and spell-

ing so you will appear professional and literate to other people who may see your message and form impressions about you, sight unseen.

"With all this advice, it's also important to remember that e-mail can 4 have some enormously positive and liberating advantages as a form of communication," Collins points out. For example, some introverted people may find it far easier to communicate electronically, as the computer medium helps them break through natural reserve. It also can help transcend cultural barriers felt by some individuals who would feel constrained from speaking in public. The convenience and inherent informality of e-mail can help cut through bureaucratic layers. Many people feel more comfortable than ever using it to communicate directly to the top, so go ahead and tell the boss what you think, but keep it brief, clear, and professional.

Questions About the Reading

1. What is the biggest mistake people make when using e-mail?
2. According to the writer, what are the eight rules to follow when writing e-mail?
3. What are the advantages of e-mail, according to Vicki Collins?

Thinking Critically

1. If you wanted to report a problem with a coworker to your supervisor and it was urgent, how would you handle it? Would you report it through e-mail?
2. What would you do if you received harassing e-mail from a coworker?

Writing Assignments

1. Suppose you have a personal problem and want to take time away from work. Write an e-mail about the situation to your supervisor.
2. A friend at work sends you an e-mail complaining about the work of another worker. Write an answer to the e-mail.

Caught in the Net

Kimberly S. Young

For some people, the Internet may become their "second home"—their virtual community— according to Kimberly S. Young. They are Internet addicts, using the Internet for escape rather than for information or communication.

Before You Read

How are you using the Internet?

Words to Know

obsessive   addicted, compulsive
panacea   remedy, cure
phenomenon   unusual or extraordinary occurrence or event
provocative   exciting, stirring
succumb   give in, submit
uninhibited   not constrained, uncontrolled

. . . The Internet is truly alive, a living, breathing electronic community. 1
For obsessive Internet users it's a second home, a special place where they feel they belong. Like the old TV show *Cheers*, the Internet becomes the place where everybody knows your name—or at least your "handle," which is the name and persona you choose to go by.

For many lonely users . . . , this second home becomes more appealing 2
than their real-life home. They become hooked on what they do and find there, dependent on the feelings they experience in this virtual community. It may be the only time they feel so free and uninhibited, so cared for and desired, so connected with others. Naturally, then, they want to use the Internet more and more to capture those good feelings and bring them into their day-to-day existence. As they chase after what stirs their deepest desires, they easily can feel tempted to kiss their old home good-bye.

Not all Internet addicts are plotting to run away and start a new life, of 3
course. But throughout my three-year study of this phenomenon, I've found that some form of escape usually lies at the heart and soul of the drive toward Internet addiction. Many of these people are depressed and lonely, held back by low self-esteem, insecurity, and anxiety. Maybe they're

181

unhappy in their relationships, or their jobs, or their social life. A few are battling diseases like cancer, or living with a permanent disability. Teenagers who succumb to the Internet's pull often say they're misunderstood by their parents and feel trapped at home.

But with the Internet, they seemingly can get away from it all. They 4 escape into a fantasyland where they make instant friends and talk any time of the day and night. From the safety of one's bedroom, office, or dorm, this electronic community emerges with remarkable ease. You don't have to get dressed up, check yourself in the mirror, or drive anywhere to meet your on-line companions. And unlike an earlier generation's experience with pen pals, you don't have to wait days or weeks for a response. With every message you type, you instantly connect with fellow users all over the world. They say something witty or provocative, you immediately answer in kind. Soon you're typing words you wouldn't dream of saying in your real life, where you may be inhibited by how people might react. In the safe haven of cyberspace, you share your deepest feelings, offer your strongest opinions, and reach out to people much faster and more openly than you would in real life.

The other people in this make-believe world can't see you, and they 5 don't know who you are. You can be whomever you choose, act however you want. If you're shy in real life, you can become outgoing on the Internet. If you're dull at a party, you can be witty in cyberspace. As one woman explained: "I can get tongue-tied in real life, but I don't get finger-tied on the Net."

If you're cautious by nature, you can take chances in cyberspace. If 6 you're considered unattractive and overweight by people who meet you in person, with a little artistic license on the Internet you can become younger and more alluring. To borrow from Garrison Keillor's description of Lake Wobegon, the Internet community becomes the place where all the women are assertive and adventuresome, all the men are blond, 25-year-old hunks, and all the children are wonderfully creative and mature beyond their years.

These Internet addicts, clearly, do not regard the Net as simply an in- 7 formational or communication tool, nor do they use it simply for enjoyment. To them, it's a form of escape that allows them to forget their problems for the time they spend on-line, much like the numbing sensation alcoholics report when they drink.

The downside, however, is that the escape is temporary. When the 8 Internet addict finally logs off for the night, the screen goes dark on the fantasy world. Real-life problems return, and now they're even harder to endure. Depression deepens, loneliness intensifies, and there's the added burden of guilt for neglecting spouse or family. That propels addicts into going on-line even more often for even longer periods of time—to find a panacea for the awakened painful feelings and to chase after the "high" they remembered from their last walk through a chat room or newsgroup. . . .

Questions About the Reading

1. What does the writer say is "at the heart and soul of the drive toward Internet addiction"?
2. What do teenagers often say is the cause of their addiction to the Internet?
3. What is the downside of Internet addiction?

Thinking Critically

1. Do you use the Internet only for e-mail? What are some other uses you think would be valuable to you personally and in your work?
2. How would you find occupational information on the Internet?

Writing Assignments

1. Search some career information Web sites to find the entrance requirements for an occupation in which you are interested. Write an e-mail report explaining the information you found and the process you used to find the information.
2. Search the Internet for information about job openings in three occupations in which you are interested. Write an essay describing the specifics of each job (skills, competencies, education, and so on) and explaining which of the jobs you would prefer and why.

bigbrother@the.office.com

Deborah Branscum

More and more corporations are tracking personal use of the Internet by their employees. Critics say it is not necessary and Deborah Branscum, in this article from Newsweek *magazine, tells us that the practice may influence the choice of employer by sought-after employees.*

Before You Read

Would it influence your choice of workplace if personal use of the Internet was prohibited?

Words to Know

cubicle   small compartment
discretion   choice, decision
laissez-faire   French for "leave-alone"

Is ESPN Sportzone on your hot list? Do you ever find yourself searching 1
for long-lost friends on Bigfoot? Watch out; your boss may want to have
a word with you.

More and more, corporations are using software tools to track employ- 2
ees' use of the Internet at the office—and managers don't always like
what they see. Products like SurfWatch Professional Edition, WebSense,
LittleBrother, and Elron Internet Manager enable companies to follow virtually every mouse click a worker makes across the Internet. They can
track access to specific Web sites and, with some programs, calculate the
corporate cost of Web-surfing slackers. Bosses can even retrieve the results of an employee's search through Internet directories such as Yahoo!
and Excite.

Corporate types say monitoring Internet usage makes workers more 3
productive, conserves network resources and helps limit legal liability
by discouraging workers from downloading objectionable material to
company computers. Critics say the practice is unnecessary, misguided,
and just plain creepy.

Employers vary widely in their policies and practices. Chevron, for 4
example, prohibits personal Internet use. Intel allows reasonable personal
use within certain guidelines and blocks employee access to sex sites. At
Hewlett-Packard (and *Newsweek*), Internet use is left to individual discretion. There is no monitoring and no blocking.

That's exactly the kind of feel-good management style that Michael   5
Sears, SurfWatch Software's general manager, would like to stamp out.
To convince companies they need SurfWatch, the company offers a free
confidential service that will analyze a company's network logs and report on the types of sites employees are visiting. Workers are "looking at
the water temperature off the coast of Maui," checking sports scores, and
tracking their stocks, says Sears—all on company time.

So what? counters Prof. Alladi Venkatesh, associate director for the   6
Center for Research on Information Technology and Organizations at the
University of California, Irvine. "What's wrong with someone checking
the water temperature in Maui?" he asks. "People go to coffee, go to the
lounge, and talk. This is one of the ways of letting off a little steam."
Some recent surveys support this laissez-faire approach. A 1997 poll of
Internet business use by the American Management Association showed
that respondents averaged 3.1 hours per week on total Internet use from
the office—and 4.1 hours of business Internet use from home. When the
Society for Human Resource Management surveyed human-resource professionals about Internet use last year, fewer than 1 percent said their
company's productivity had decreased greatly. More than 45 percent said
productivity had gone up.

In a few years, worry about Internet abuse will have faded, as it has   7
about other technologies, Venkatesh says. In the meantime, people often
get access to the Internet without much training and need to experiment
to learn how to use the Net effectively. Employers may view this as goof-
ing off, but people are simply getting used to something new, says
Venkatesh. Managers shouldn't overreact by monitoring, which is itself a
waste of company resources and one more distraction for busy managers.

At Chevron, for example, the department responsible for monitoring   8
Internet usage classified the CNN Interactive site in its nonbusiness category. "A lot of us get good news from CNN," says Chevron spokesper-
son Alison Jones. "Nonbusiness is a matter of opinion. We have no way
of knowing exactly how each individual person gets business value from
each individual site—unless we go door to door to ask them, and Lord
knows we don't have time for that."

The issue is further complicated as the lines between work time and   9
leisure time continue to blur. It's now typical for employees to be on call
via beeper or cell phone beyond 9 to 5, and business travel often requires
employees to spend weekends away from home. Dilbert cartoonist and
avid cybersurfer Scott Adams says, "It's gotten to the point where the
only place you can get work done is at home, because no one bugs you,
and the best place to entertain yourself is at work, because the Internet

connections are faster." As it happens, the Dilbert Zone comic site is blocked by SurfWatch. "The world has turned inside out, but not all employers are ready to handle that," says Adams.

Cubicle dwellers may get their revenge. Adams's upcoming book, "The 10 Joy of Work," recommends that his readers—often brainy, highly sought-after engineers—avoid employers who monitor Internet usage. Robert Kelley, a Carnegie-Mellon professor and author of "How to Be a Star at Work," says that may become more common. Eventually, Internet monitoring will "become a sorting tool in terms of what kind of employees you can attract and retain," he says. Take that, Big Brother.

Questions About the Reading

1. What reasons do corporations give for tracking employee use of the Internet?
2. What are the objections critics have to a corporation tracking employee Internet use?
3. What were the results of the poll by the American Management Association regarding employee business use of the Internet at home and in the office?
4. What were the results of the Society for Human Resource Management survey regarding the effect of Internet use on company productivity?
5. What has been the influence of beepers and cell phones on workers?

Thinking Critically

1. Do you think companies should screen objectionable materials and Web sites from their computers? Why or why not?
2. If a company wants to screen objectionable materials and Web sites from its computers, who should decide what is objectionable?

Writing Assignments

1. Suppose your company wants to screen certain Web sites from its computers. Working with classmates, decide the criteria to be used in choosing the sites to screen. Write an informal report in letter form explaining the criteria and the process used to determine the criteria.
2. Write an e-mail to your supervisor suggesting guidelines for personal use of the Internet by employees.

Saying Adios to the Office

Edward C. Baig

Technology, a strong economy, and employees who must combine careers, family, and personal needs have combined to increase the number of persons working at home. But there are guidelines the successful telecommuter needs to follow, according to Edward C. Baig.

Before You Read

What do you think are the advantages and disadvantages of telecommuting?

Words to Know

assuage   ease, satisfy, relieve

demarcate   define, set out

imperative   essential, vital

intranets   computer network connections within a company or group

telecommuting   traveling and/or communicating by telephone, cable, and computer technology for business purposes

———

Now that her commute to the office lasts all of 10 seconds, Vicki Hall 1 has lots of time on her hands. A senior communications analyst for Visa International, Hall used to drive some $2^1/2$ hours each day to and from Visa's San Francisco headquarters. After moving to Pensacola, Fla., Hall, a single mother, is still taking care of business. With the blessing of her California bosses and armed with a company-paid, PC, fax, ISDN phone line, and storage shelves, Hall has turned a spare bedroom into an office. "Telecommuting gave me my life back," she says.

As professional men and women attempt to do justice to their careers 2 while attending to family and personal needs, more and more are working without visiting the office more than once in a blue moon. The appeal is enormous. At home, you can spend more time with the kids, work in casual clothes, and tailor a schedule that lets you tackle your job at odd hours. Some 9.9 million people work outside their main corporate offices at least three days a month, up from 9.1 million in 1997 and 5.4 million in 1993, according to Raymond Boggs, director of home-office research for International Data Corp. in Framingham, Mass.

Telecommuting has gotten an added boost from a strong economy in 3
which employers must make accommodations to attract the best and
brightest workers. There are also environmental and political pressures
as companies respond to Clean Air Act provisions that aim to cut traffic.
And businesses want to pare real estate costs by creating "hoteling" arrangements in which, say, 10 people share a single cubicle on an as-needed
basis. Companies are finding that telecommuting can boost productivity
5% to 20%, according to Jack M. Nilles, author of *Managing Telework*. . . .

Technology is helping people break free of the office. With laptops, 4
speedy modems, the Internet, and the emergence of corporate intranets,
jobs are becoming portable. Employers and employees can easily swap
e-mail and share PC documents from afar. This cuts down on faxing and
overnight-courier costs.

Is telecommuting for you? Nearly 75% of teleworkers responding to 5
an AT&T survey last year said they were more satisfied with their personal and family lives than before they started working at home. But
telecommuting is not for every person or job, and you'll need a massive
dose of self-discipline to pull it off. Ask yourself if you can perform your
duties without the boss breathing down your neck. On the other hand,
would you go stir-crazy without being able to shmooze with officemates?

Many companies insist that you iron out a schedule with your super- 6
visor before you begin. You may prefer to work at 6 A.M. and hit the links
at 3 P.M.—just be sure you're available for those 9 A.M. meetings. Not every
company will require formal training before you set up a remote office,
but it's a good idea to sound out your boss about his or her concerns.

Appearances count. It's equally smart to assuage the fears of coworkers. 7
Your colleagues may become resentful if they think you're on paid vacation or suspect they'll get saddled with extra work in your absence. As a
result, you may want to trade favors with your cohorts—by covering for
them if they leave early one day, for example. And make sure they know
they can call you at home. Appearances count: If you choose to work two
days a week at home, you may not want to make them Monday and Fri-
day, advises telecommuting consultant Gil Gordon in Monmouth Junc-
tion, N.J. Peers might think you're taking long weekends.

It's also imperative to set up ground rules with your family. The good 8
news about telecommuting is that you can be close to your loved ones.
That's also the bad news. Spouses and small children have to understand
that even though you're in the house, you are busy earning a living. It's
fine to throw in a few loads of laundry or answer the door when the
plumber comes. It's another thing to take the kids to the mall or let them
play games on your office PC.

Clearly demarcate your workspace by using a separate room with a 9
door you can shut. Let your family know that, emergencies excepted, the

space is off-limits during working hours. Some employees wear corporate badges or business attire at home to alert the family that they do not want to be disturbed.

If you have infants or toddlers, arrange for child care. Telecommuting 10 is not a substitute for dependent care," says Barbara M. Reeves, a virtual-office program manager for Boeing. "With a young child, you're really trying to hold down two jobs—and probably not doing very well with either one."

Once you get down to business, you may have to work hard to remain 11 in the loop. That's why so many telecommuters stay at home only a couple of days a week. Aside from rubbing elbows with bosses and cohorts, there are meetings and other situations where face time is essential. Just one in five telecommuters responding to the AT&T study indicated that they felt more isolated working at home. But some teleworkers worry that being out of sight means being out of mind, and that that will hurt their chances for a promotion or a bonus. Moreover, you may be concerned that if bad times hit, you'll be the first to get sacked.

Be a star. The best way to eliminate such concerns is to produce. "You 12 need to establish your credibility," says Betty Sun, who works from her house in Bethesda, Md., as an acquisitions editor for publisher John Wiley & Sons in New York. Of course, while it's important to put in a full day of work while telecommuting, also remember that there's a time to leave the office. When the lines between your home and office blur, it can be hard to pull yourself away.

Maintaining the balance has not been a problem for Sun. She has been 13 promoted since she began telecommuting and now manages two New York employees from a distance. But there may come a time when you'll have to ponder a difficult question: Would you rather climb the corporate ladder or the stairs to your home office? The higher up you move in your organization, the more likely it is that your presence at headquarters may be required at all times. Telecommuting can be terrific at certain stages of your life and career. But when the kids are older, you may be ready to return to the office full-time.

Even though the telecommuting phenomenon continues to mushroom, 14 you may still encounter old-fashioned employers who are resisting the trend. But if you're a star performer, lots of companies will let you telecommute if that's the way to hook you. "The whole drift of the '90s is to introduce flexibility into work flow," says Thomas E. Miller, a vice-president for Cyber Dialogue, a New York–based research and consulting firm. That's good to know if you find the back-and-forth pull of train or car commuting is pulling you apart at the seams.

Questions About the Reading

1. What is the main idea of the article?
2. What has boosted the willingness of companies to establish telecommuting for their employees?
3. How many people were working outside their corporate offices when the article was written in 1998?
4. What were the results of the AT&T survey of telecommuting workers?
5. What should a person do to set up an office at home?

Thinking Critically

1. What personal competencies do you think it would take to be a successful telecommuter?
2. What are the advantages and disadvantages of working in an office? What are they for working at home?
3. Would you prefer to work at home or in an office? Why?

Writing Assignments

1. Write an e-mail to your supervisor asking for a meeting to discuss telecommuting.
2. Using the suggestions in the article, write a memo to your supervisor regarding telecommuting.
3. Develop a line graph using the statistics in paragraph 2.

8

Managing Your Life

So you have decided on your career, finished school, and know the family and work-related issues you may face. But do you know how to manage your life? It's time to think and plan ahead.

No matter what your career or how many different careers you have, Tim O'Brien's advice is to "Set a Course for Lifelong Learning." He suggests taking advantage of all the information available in books, magazines, newspapers, and the Internet to keep yourself up-to-date in your present career and to learn about technological and other changes that may affect your future.

But what if you find that the career you have chosen is not satisfying you? Cassandra Hayes offers some advice in "Stop the World, I Want to Get Off" for knowing when it's time to change careers. Kathleen Green points out in "Traditional Degrees, Nontraditional Jobs: A Degree Is Not a Life Sentence" that, instead of changing careers altogether, some people manage to combine successfully their traditional career training with work they love.

And don't forget to plan, beginning now, not just for your work, family, and financial security but also for how you will spend your time after retirement. In "What Will You Do When You Retire?" Ralph Warner provides some important suggestions and advice.

In this chapter, you will prepare a résumé, write a cover letter to accompany the résumé, and write a thank you letter.

The Résumé

The following information must be included in a résumé:

> Name, address, telephone number (fax number and e-mail address are optional)
> Education
> Experience

Other information can include your career objective, honors, activities, and references. Your career objective should be like the description of the job you are seeking. If you list any names as references, you must first ask each person you are listing if she or he will be willing to supply a reference for you and provide them with a description of the position you are seeking. An example of a résumé follows.

Kristin Smith Guenov

425 College Ave., Apt. 3L
Orono, ME 04473
(207) 866-4085
Kristin_Guenov@career.umeadm.maine.edu

Objective

Employment in the career services field.

Qualifications

- Strong written and oral communication ability
- Excellent computer skills
- One year's experience in Career Services

Education

M.Ed., Student Development in Higher Education (expected 8/96)
University of Maine, Orono, ME

- Concentration in Administration
- 3.95 GPA
- Full-tuition Trustee Scholarship

B.A., Anthropology (5/89)
Wellesley College, Wellesley, MA

- Concentration in Chinese and Linguistics
- Cum Laude
- Junior Year Abroad—University of Edinburgh

Relevant Experience

Career Center, University of Maine, Orono, ME

Graduate Career Assistant (9/94–present)

- Design and implement World Wide Web pages for both the UMaine Career Center and the campus Peace Corps Office.
- Conduct résumé critiques, both in the Career Center and at a weekly résumé review booth at the Student Union.
- Assist students in accessing career-related information via print media and the Internet.

Peace Corps Representative (9/94–9/95)
- Established new Peace Corps Office on campus.
- Promoted Peace Corps via World Wide Web site, campus BBS, and campus-wide posters.
- Conducted preliminary interviews with prospective applicants and disseminated Peace Corps information.

Other Experience

Husson College, Bangor, ME (1991–1994)
ESL Instructor

- Provided intensive ESL instruction to students from a wide variety of language backgrounds.
- Collaborated with fellow instructors on curriculum development and program enhancement.

Garden Hotel, Shanghai, China (1990–1991)
ESL Instructor

- Initiated and implemented English language program for newly opened, five-star Japanese hotel.

- Worked independently, with only minimal supervision.
- Conferred closely with both Chinese and Japanese management to increase program effectiveness.

Shanghai Fisheries University, Shanghai, China (1989–1990)
ESL Instructor

- Taught English reading, listening, and conversation classes to both undergraduate and graduate students.
- Gained an awareness and an appreciation of the Chinese culture.

Additional Information

- Experience with both IBM PCs and Macintosh computers.
- Proficient in MS Word 6.0, QuickMail, HTML.edit, Netscape, First Class Client, and PowerPoint 4.0.
- Limited knowledge of Mandarin Chinese and Bulgarian.

The Cover Letter

A cover letter is generally but not always sent with your résumé. Although you may not be comfortable selling yourself as much as the applicant does in the following example, it is important to remember that the purpose of a cover letter is to point out that your training and experience meet the requirements of the position for which you are applying and to persuade the employer to grant you an interview.

Ms. Linda Smith
734 Chestnut Avenue
Lewistown, MA 02345
(617) 123-4567

October 24, 1996

Ms. Cheryl Johnson
Vice President
State Street Investment Bank
211 State Street
Spring City, MA 04321

Dear Ms. Johnson:

The teller position described in your recent <u>Daily Record</u> advertisement immediately caught my attention. My proven track record working for a financial institution makes me an ideal candidate for the job, and I have enclosed my résumé for your consideration. You will find that my qualifications exceed your requirements.

For example, you specify that you are looking for someone with customer service skills and experience handling money. While attending college I worked for my university's credit union for two years. While there I handled cash transactions, opened accounts, prepared general ledger entries, took loan payments, cashed checks, and took deposits. I am a skilled team player with exemplary customer service skills.

I look forward to discussing the position with you in more detail. If you feel that my qualifications are as much a match for State Street Investment Bank as I feel they are, please call me at your earliest convenience to schedule an interview. I look forward to hearing from you and thank you for your consideration.

Sincerely,

Linda Smith
enc.

The Thank You Letter

If you are fortunate enough to have an interview with the prospective employer, don't forget your manners. Send a thank you letter (see the following example) that expresses your appreciation for the interview and, assuming the chance of employment is still open, briefly reviews your qualifications for the job. Even if you are not successful in getting the job, send a thank you letter anyway. You never know whether another job opportunity will come up with the company, and the person who interviewed you is apt to remember that you had the courtesy to send a thank you!

Ms. Cheryl Johnson
Vice President
State Street Investment Bank
211 State Street
Spring City, MA 04321

Dear Ms. Johnson:

Thank you for taking the time to meet with me today regarding the teller position at State Street Investment Bank. I am particularly excited about the opportunity. As we discussed, my qualifications closely match the requirements you have for the position. In addition, two years in my university's credit union have given me experience handling cash transactions and dealing with customers—traits you stressed as being important in your candidates.

If there is any way I can be of further assistance in the decision process, please feel free to give me a call. I look forward to hearing from you again shortly. Again, I appreciate your consideration.

Sincerely,

Linda Smith

Set a Course for Lifelong Learning

Tim O'Brien

Just because you have finished school and have a job, you should not stop learning. Tim O'Brien explains that everyone should have a plan for lifelong learning.

Before You Read

You use all the latest technology. But do you know how to change a flat tire on your car?

Words to Know

complacent   smug, self-satisfied
innovation   change, new method or device
intricate   complicated
myriad   many

"**I**'m done learning!" When I heard this several years ago, I nearly gasped 1
aloud. The person who said it was a successful salesman. He had completed several of the most intricate land transactions I'd ever seen.

I asked him what he meant by being done learning. "I know every- 2
thing I need to know about selling. All I have to do now is get the details and I come up with the solution in a few minutes."

Now, about seven years later, that man isn't as successful as he was 3
when he made the "done learning" statement. In several ways, the world has passed him by. Right now, he's trying to become computer literate. He has realized that if he wants to compete today with the young men and women in real estate, he has to use technology. He still doesn't want to use a beeper or cellular phone. He knows he should have a Web page and e-mail for the convenience of his customers. However, it nearly causes him physical pain to put in the time to learn these new devices.

He knows now that he should have developed a plan for continuous 4
learning and upgrading of his skills. If he had, he wouldn't be so far behind today. He realizes that his drop in income relates directly to his failing to keep up with the changes we all face.

My friend isn't alone. We all know someone like him. If you are older 5
than 35, chances are high that you might be what the younger people call

"techno-phobes." However, it isn't only technology that we need to keep up with. It is also the myriad of changes in every aspect of life.

We have a choice. We can broaden the scope of ways in which we keep 6 in touch with the world around us. Or we risk becoming isolated and so specialized in our knowledge that we can only communicate with others in our field.

Many people argue that the age of the "universal person" is over. Ac- 7 tually, I'd argue that it is even more important now. To succeed, we must have as broad as possible exposure to as many areas as you can learn about. The world's knowledge now doubles about every five years. Soon it will be every three years. That's impressive. It's also an opportunity to expand yourself.

The more input you have from many varied sources, the better your 8 chance of recognizing patterns or gaps. This will allow you to capitalize on them by providing information or services concerning those patterns or gaps. Faith Popcorn and Gerald Celente both make large incomes while providing valuable services as futurists. They gather information from thousands of sources. They look for patterns. Then they think what those patterns imply. Their predictions on future trends are often very accurate.

Make a plan for yourself to become a futurist. Begin to gather informa- 9 tion from wide and varied sources. "Read odd stuff. Talk to unusual people. Spend half of your time out of the office. And spend half of that time with whackos" as Tom Peters, the innovation specialist, puts it. The idea is to get you to think and consider all the life that exists outside your normal experiences. Read magazines by people or groups you disagree with. I've found this to be a very good way for me to face my preconceptions, opinions, and biases about the groups involved.

There has never been so much information available to us. Take ad- 10 vantage of it through books, magazines, newspapers, and the Internet. The more we learn, the more information and resources we have available to us to make informed decisions. It will also keep you out in front of nearly everyone else you know. Too many people become complacent and, at some point, feel they've "got it made." At that moment they begin to fall behind. Remember the law of entropy. "That which does not grow, begins to die."

Questions About the Reading

1. What should the salesman have done to maintain his ability to compete with others in real estate?

2. How often does the world's knowledge now double?
3. What is a futurist? Explain what futurists do and how they do it.

Thinking Critically

1. What current events magazines do you read? What do you think is the political bias of each magazine?
2. What books have you read in the past year? Were the books on the same or different subjects?

Writing Assignments

1. In your journal, list three subjects you would like to know more about.
2. Using your journal list, write an informal report of the sources (books, magazines, the Internet) you could use to learn more about the subjects.

Stop the World, I Want to Get Off

Cassandra Hayes

Disappointment in their chosen work, job insecurity, and stress cause workers to want to change careers, according to Cassandra Hayes. She offers ten signs to help you know if it is time to make a career change and advice on how to prepare for that change.

Before You Read

What are your expectations from your career? What would make you want to change careers?

Words to Know

apprehensive   uneasy, fearful
dehumanized   deprived of human qualities
demeaned   humbled, lowered in dignity or stature
dominate   control, rule
sabbatical   period of rest, time away from regular duties

. . . Longer hours, increased responsibility, and little free time have cre- 1
ated a legion of stressed-out workers with no real outlet. Others have found that the grind of a nine-to-five job no longer offers them all they thought it would.

"It's part of the natural evolution of human beings to want to feel that 2
their work is valuable and that they are making a contribution," says James C. Gonyea, founder and host of the American Online Career Center in New Port Richey, Florida. "As people move higher up in an organization, they become distanced from the people they were intended to serve. They begin to feel unfulfilled."

Another reason some individuals want to change their line of work is 3
the realization that they were in the wrong field to begin with. So many people are not fully aware of their interests, abilities, values, and needs— those elements that make up their personality type. "It is very difficult to identify occupations that are right for you if you're unsure about who you are," states Gonyea. "Unfortunately, the realization that you're in the wrong job doesn't usually come until after you've been there for a while, which in time leads some to make a change."

Still others have grown tired of the threat to financial and career secu- 4
rity that decades of downsizing have brought. Many have sought refuge

200

in entrepreneurship or family matters. Meanwhile, technology has created new possibilities and careers that were only imagined five years ago, opening the door to new vocational possibilities, says Gonyea.

Stress is a major reason for discontent in the workplace and costs employers an estimated $150 billion to $200 billion annually, according to the Society for Human Resource Management in Alexandria, Virginia. In response, more companies are recognizing that employees are more productive if they are given a chance to periodically take time off while focusing on personal priorities.   5

As a result, sabbaticals are becoming popular. They allow employees time to reflect on their careers and the overall operation of the business, away from the daily pressures of the office. With a three-, six-, or twelve-month leave, employees get a break from job stress, and employers get workers who return refreshed and ready to go.   6

Spot the Signs

So how do you really know when it's time to make a change? Gonyea offers 10 common road signs. You're feeling: 7

- bored and unchallenged;
- demeaned and dehumanized;
- as though you're working well beyond your capabilities;
- like an outcast around your coworkers;
- burnt out from emotionally exhausting work;
- seriously and consistently underpaid;
- extensively overqualified;
- unrecognized or unrewarded for your labor;
- that your boss is unrealistic or overly demanding;
- that the job offers little room for personal or professional growth.

If most of these points apply to you, then a change may be in order.   8

Devise a Game Plan

The good news: making a change is possible. The bad news: it isn't easy. There is clearly some risk, since few people can shift career gears on a whim and be successful. Therefore you must develop a strategy. Whatever you choose to do, part of that game plan must involve getting your finances in order. That may mean paying off all debt, building a nest egg to last you six months to a year and curtailing expenses. If you're worrying about paying the rent, it's hard to focus on your dreams. Your survival needs cannot dominate your long-term goals.   9

Look inside yourself to be sure of what you want. Preparing the ground- 10
work entails headwork, legwork, and paperwork. You must decide on
the specifics of your leave, and do some in-depth research into its costs,
benefits, and personal and professional feasibility. All in all, consider these
goals when negotiating with yourself:

- Determine how much time you want off;
- Establish a budget and pay off any outstanding bills;
- Discuss your decision with family and friends who may be apprehensive of your motives; and
- Set down objectives by asking yourself what you want to accomplish. Just because you are not in the office doesn't mean you're
  not working. You still need to have goals. . . .

Questions About the Reading

1. According to the writer, what is the major reason for discontent in the
   workplace?
2. Why have companies started providing sabbaticals for their employees?
3. What are the road signs that indicate a person should make a career
   change?
4. What are the steps a person should take to prepare for a leave from
   work or career change?

Thinking Critically

1. What are your expectations from your choice of careers in terms of
   responsibility, status, working hours, vacations, and income?
2. If you had a friend who was really stressed out over his or her working situation, what would you do to help? What would you advise
   him or her to do?

Writing Assignments

1. Suppose you have been working as an accountant for several years
   but are dissatisfied with conditions at your company. Create your educational and working history and prepare a résumé to apply for a position at another company.
2. Write a cover letter to enclose with your résumé.

Traditional Degrees, Nontraditional Jobs:
A Degree Is Not a Life Sentence

Kathleen Green

If the work your traditional degree prepares you for doesn't quite satisfy you, don't despair. Kathleen Green provides examples of three persons who used their traditional degree training in careers that have made them happy.

Before You Read

What are the different jobs for which your degree qualifies you?

Words to Know

disgruntled   disagreeable, dissatisfied

embark   start, begin

ensure   guarantee

forte   strength

honing   sharpening

launching   entering, starting

prerequisite   prior requirement

... Before you start a new job, you probably have ideas about what you 1
want your work life to be like. Your expectations might concern the amount
of responsibility you will have, how much say you'll have in major decisions involving your efforts, the number of hours you'll be expected to
work, and so forth. You may also have, in the back of your mind, a personal deadline for moving on if reality clashes with your hopes.

At some point in your career, though, you might decide to choose be- 2
tween staying in a job that is secure but unsatisfying—or taking a risk on
something else that is more closely aligned with your passions. It may
take awhile for your dream job to become reality; after all, rookies are
expected to pay their dues. But as the following examples illustrate, staying focused on an ideal can lead to rewarding results.

Once a Nurse, Always a Nurse

"Ever since I was a little girl, I've always been fascinated by other cul- 3
tures," says nurse entrepreneur Dotti Dasher-Riddle. "And I've always

203

been very committed to continuing education, even though it's not required by many states for nursing."

So, after earning a diploma in nursing and working as an emergency 4
room nurse and developing college continuing education programs,
Dasher-Riddle had an idea for something new. "I took all of my passions
in life—my vocation and my avocations—and rolled them into one," she
says. "I asked myself, 'What do I want to do? Where do I want to go?'"
The answers to those questions convinced her to start her own company,
HealthCare GLOBE (Global Learning Opportunities for Broadening Education), Inc., which provides international continuing education experiences for health care professionals. . . .

Redesigning an Engineer

Paul Floreck knew at an early age what he wanted to be when he grew 5
up. "I wanted to be an engineer," he says, "and I was always fascinated
by airplanes." Earning a bachelor's degree in aerospace engineering, followed by a master's in mechanical engineering, were educational steps
to fulfilling that flight of fancy.

Floreck worked for about a decade in the aerospace industry, primar- 6
ily on the west coast, holding engineering jobs as a designer and analyst.
But he wanted to live closer to family on the east coast, so he took a position in New Jersey as a consultant in the rail transportation industry. Eighteen months later, about the time he realized the rail industry was not his
forte, he noticed a *New York Times* want ad for a person who could provide sales staff with technical information on an aircraft company's products. "I really wanted the job, and I knew the competition would be tough,"
says Floreck. "I took the ad apart and made sure my résumé showed
every bit of my experience directly relevant to the position." His strategy
worked; he got the job. . . .

Practice Not Perfect for All Lawyers

Like many people who become lawyers, Jim Doerfler had thought about 7
it long before college and started honing his skills to prepare for it. "I had
always considered law school," he says. "My high school had a strong
speech and debate program, and I took part in that and competed at the
state and national levels." He also did some debating in college. After
graduating from law school, he worked for a judge and then for a law
firm, where he defended large corporate clients in civil lawsuits.

Meanwhile, Doerfler's father and his father's business partner in an 8
electrical subcontracting business started talking about retirement. And

Doerfler starting thinking about taking over their business. "I was assessing my career options," he says, "and the idea of having my own business, especially continuing into the future something that had already been established, was very appealing to me." He quit his job at the law firm and began working at the family business as a project manager and cost estimator. Now, the owner-partners are negotiating a deal to turn the business over to their sons.

"I didn't think about going into the family business until I was out in 9 the working world, where I was faced with issues like downsizing and job security," says Doerfler. "I started thinking that the best of all possible worlds is the family business. It allows you to do as much as you're capable of. I wanted to do something different and continue what's been done before." . . .

Not Just a Job: Changing Careers for Love of Work

Don't despair if you feel you have made a wrong career move. But instead of simply staying put and being miserable, take steps to move your career in the right direction. . . . 10

Knowing what your skills and interests are will help you determine 11 which jobs you would like to do. . . . Once you identify your skills and interests, figure out how they help you become marketable in the work force. . . .

Anyone thinking about making a career change should plan on doing 12 a lot of exercises in areas like self-assessment, ranking priorities, and setting goals. But people with specialized skills have additional considerations. Your training might be narrowly tailored; . . . education for occupations such as nurse, engineer, and lawyer does not always leave room for broad-based electives. Careful assessment of your skills and knowledge will help you determine what courses, if any, you need to take before embarking on a new career.

Even if you take a few classes leading toward a new career, try to ensure that the direction you plan to take is one you really want to pursue. 13 Volunteering or working part time provides a test run for finding out how well the expertise you have combines with your craving to do something else. It's better to discover that you lack acting ability when you are in community theater than after you've quit your job. Volunteer and part-time jobs, like internships, can also help prepare you for your new career. . . .

Convincing an employer that you have what it takes to do a job always 14 requires preparation. But when it comes to pursuing a new career field, you may have some additional explaining to do. . . . Demonstrate to potential employers your enthusiasm, self-confidence, resourcefulness, flexibility, perseverance, and commitment to a new career direction. . . .

The better you ready yourself to move into a new field, the more sure 15
you will be of your decision to change careers. Self-doubt might be one of
the biggest hurdles you have to overcome, especially since there are no
guarantees the doubt will evaporate when you embark on your new career. Feeling confident about your calling, however, makes it easier to be
comfortable that the decision is right for you. . . .

Self-Defeating Career Strategies:
Are You Your Worst Enemy?

One of the first things to determine when considering changing career 16
fields is whether you're genuinely unsatisfied with your career choice or
just unhappy with your job. Deciding to change jobs is one thing; launching into a completely new field is another. Almost all workers experience
highs and lows in their jobs. The key is to recognize when you're in a
normal rut—and when a drastic career move is the only way to improve
your outlook.

But don't be too quick to start marching to the beat of a disgruntled 17
drummer. Carefully evaluate your options, skills, knowledge, and interests; otherwise, you might find yourself searching for the perfect career
when all you really want is a better job in your field. If you've adopted
some or all of the following tactics, it is likely you are unsure about your
decision to change career fields:

- Deciding from the outset that you must earn the same amount of
  money or maintain the same level of status, responsibility, or prestige in your next job. Humility is an important trait for easing the
  trauma of job change, especially if you are planning a move from
  a prestigious job to a fresh start in a new field.
- Getting another educational degree when it isn't a requirement
  for the type of work you'd like to do. Investigate your target industry to determine whether a specialized advanced degree is an
  absolute prerequisite—or just another of your attempts to post-
  pone making a career decision. Apprenticing in the field for a year
  might go as far as the 2 or 3 years and thousands of dollars you
  could spend on more schooling. On the other hand, don't rule out
  taking a class or two if you feel it would be helpful for your new
  venture.
- Trying to do something about your career only when you're feeling unhappy with it. Do you make a half-hearted attempt to find
  another job only when things get tough at work, then shelve those
  plans when work pressure eases up? Most career counselors agree
  that an effective career search must continue through the good

times and that it requires stamina and commitment equal to at least a part-time job.

- Waiting for opportunities to fall in your lap. You may feel you've paid your dues and should be able to reap the benefits from all your hard work. Better get used to the idea that making contacts and building an image are an ongoing process, not a finite one.
- Believing that you'll only be hired to do something for which you have been formally trained or educated. You have skills; it's up to you to translate those skills into something marketable. Be creative in figuring out ways to transfer your knowledge, interests, and experience into another field.
- Keeping your feelings of dissatisfaction to yourself, or dumping them only on your family. This is one time you need to surround yourself with people you can relate to. Seek others who have made a successful career change, and use their examples to find solutions to your own problems. Look for support from people who are undergoing a similar experience. In short, find the allies you need to complete your transition.
- Expecting your work life to bring you complete personal fulfillment. One theory holds that each person's sense of satisfaction relies on fulfillment in four areas: Work, relationships, leisure, and challenge. Instead of expecting work to satisfy all four elements, figure out how you meet your needs in the other three; then evaluate your job.
- Slamming doors shut behind you. Don't bad-mouth the coworkers, boss, or profession you left. The quality of your past work and the relationships you developed there are the keys to obtaining future employment.
- Holding onto the belief that you owe a lifetime commitment to your current employer, your next job, or even to your career field. Think in terms of building experience over the long term, rather than looking at each job as a 35-year commitment.
- Staying where you are because you're afraid of failing. Fear of the unknown may keep you from evaluating your likes and dislikes or from facing up to the fact that you might not achieve the success you crave in your field. But retirement regrets could be worse.

Questions About the Reading

1. What is the main idea of the article?
2. What does the writer say a person should do to prepare for a career change?
3. What does the writer say are a person's worst enemies when he or she makes a career change?

Thinking Critically

1. How would you proceed if you wanted to change jobs but also wanted to use the degree training you have?
2. How would you proceed if you were unable to find a job in the field for which you were trained?

Writing Assignments

1. Choose a help-wanted advertisement from your local newspaper and prepare a résumé to apply for the position. Include a cover letter.
2. Assume that you have had an interview for the position. Write a thank you letter to the person who interviewed you.
3. Assume that you had an interview for the position and have been told the position has been filled by someone else. Write a thank you letter to the person who interviewed you.

What Will You Do When You Retire?

Ralph Warner

It's never too soon to start planning for your retirement. Even if you've done your financial planning, you should consider also how you will spend your time.

Before You Read

Do you do any volunteer work or have a hobby?

Words to Know

crucial vital, significant
karmic pertaining to the concept of destiny
meager small, scant
unprecedented unheard of, never before

Ask people about their retirement planning, and they are likely to tick 1
off their financial investments. That's all well and good, but it ignores
another crucial aspect of retirement planning: figuring out how they will
spend their time.

Many Americans will live from one-quarter to one-third of their lives 2
after age 65. In my observation, most people—especially those who have
been busy earlier in life—make the transition to a fulfilling retirement if,
and only if, they stay busy. I can't find anyone in their 60s and 70s who
says it's fun to spend their days watching TV, sitting on a park bench,
sleeping late, or even just reading.

Start Planning Now

Lots of people in midlife—especially those whose lives center on their 3
work—avoid thinking about retirement because they just can't picture
what they'll do. As one mid-level manager told me, "Once they take away
my employee ID number, I'm not sure what I'll do or how I'll define
myself."

Why worry about retirement activities now, when retirement is years, 4
or even decades, away? Because, put bluntly, people who count on developing new interests and involvements after 65 often don't. Fred Astaire
had it about right when he said, "Old age is like everything else. To make

a success of it, you've got to start young." Just as a passive approach to financial planning usually means a meager bank balance, failure to look ahead at what you will do when you retire may mean a bored, depressed old age.

What will you do when you retire? Take a few minutes to write down 5 the things you expect to be actively involved in. Don't count solo activities such as reading, watching TV, or jogging. While fine in themselves, they are not likely to keep you energized and interesting for long. Be as specific as you can. For example, if you plan to participate in charitable activities aimed at helping educate Third World children, who will you work with and what will you do?

In my experience, too many people list things like travel, adult educa- 6 tion courses, and golf and then get stuck. Sorry, but participating in a couple of activities won't be enough to keep you interested in life and interesting to others. Ideally, to avoid boredom—and even more important, to avoid boring others—you will want to participate in a number of interests and activities.

If you're having trouble thinking what these will be, don't panic. But 7 you do need to do some more thinking and investigating about what your life may be like after retirement. Here are some possibilities:

Working Part-Time

Many people who enjoy the bustle and creativity of the workplace find 8 that working at least part-time after retirement age offers the best opportunity to stay busily involved in life. And, of course, working a few extra years can go a long way toward helping solve money problems. As of 1990, paychecks were the second largest source of income, after Social Security, for Americans between 65 and 74, according to the Department of Labor.

But will work be available? Despite laws prohibiting discrimination 9 on the basis of age, it isn't always easy for an older person to find a part-time job that is both interesting and moderately well-paying. This is likely to be doubly true for baby boomers, who will be retiring in unprecedented numbers and competing for work.

Certainly if you hope to establish a new career—or even find a part- 10 time job more challenging than flipping burgers or taking tickets at an amusement park—it's a good idea to think, well in advance, about how you are going to make it happen. And if you come up with what sounds like a sensible plan, do all you can to test whether it's really likely to work. Just because you think you would enjoy teaching, working in a plant nursery, or caring for small children doesn't mean anyone will hire you to do it, or if they do, that you will find it satisfying.

Anyone who wants to turn a hobby—for example, designing gardens— 11 into a business needs to do lots of homework. Many years spent learning about plants and how to create lovely landscapes won't be enough.

To run a successful landscape business, a gardener also needs to know, 12 among other things, how to market her services, buy wholesale, hire help for heavy digging and lifting, bill for services, and collect accounts. Learning those skills may mean cutting back current work and, as a result, forgoing short-term income.

Volunteering

An active, maybe even passionate, involvement with good causes can be 13 hugely positive for anyone. For older people, especially those who already have enough income, volunteering can be particularly satisfying for several reasons, including these:

- **A chance to do interesting work:** In the private sector, companies are busy trying to make money. Nothing wrong with that, except it means their employees must stick with the program, which is unlikely to involve all sorts of fascinating endeavors. For example, not many corporations work to preserve a forest, record oral histories of elderly immigrants, or teach children to read. But nonprofit organizations are active in all these—and hundreds of other—fascinating areas.
- **A way to add meaning to life:** In addition, knowing that you are doing good and needed work can give your life far more meaning than it might otherwise have. Working to improve the quality of life helps some people cope with the inevitability of their own death.
- **A way to pay one's karmic debts:** Working with nonprofits gives people the chance to indirectly repay those whose efforts have smoothed their own way. Whether it be a grandparent, teacher, or older friend, we all know and cherish the memories of people who helped or enriched our own lives or paved our way. Helping others gives many older people the feeling that they are passing on the love and support once given them.
- **An opportunity to meet interesting people:** Regular workplaces are great places to make friends, too, but nonprofit groups tend to attract like-minded people—people interested in adult literacy or bilingual education, or reptiles. Finding people you can truly bond with may be easier.

Planning ahead can be key to succeeding as a volunteer. At first you 14 may think this is silly—after all, you're not asking to be paid, only to help out. Think again. Increasingly, bigger nonprofits rely on paid staff to accomplish many day-to-day tasks, using only a small group of knowledgeable volunteers to staff the board of directors and advisory committees. People who know the field and have up-to-date skills are in great demand, but those who have little to offer beyond a desire to help may have a hard time finding satisfying work.

But couldn't you always begin with a simple task, such as answering 15 the phone, until you figure out a more exciting way to get involved? Don't be so sure. Rapid technological change is squeezing out unskilled tasks in the nonprofit sector only slightly more slowly than in corporate America. For example, with the recent marriage of phones and computers, even taking or forwarding a message can be a daunting task.

The lesson is the same as it is in the profit-making sector: explore your 16 hoped-for nonprofit career well before you retire and actually need it.

For example, one friend, Joan, had planned for years to help out with a 17 marine animal rescue project. She retired early to begin, but was hugely disappointed to discover that being around cold salt water made her arthritis flare up so badly that she couldn't continue. And for various reasons, her volunteer efforts with several other wildlife organizations didn't work out. Joan finally found a good match at the animal lab at a children's science museum—and feels lucky things worked out so well.

Exploring Hobbies

For lots of people, retirement is a chance to finally be able to do things 18 they have put off all their lives. If this describes you, I have an important question to ask: Outside of your work and family, where do you now spend a significant amount of time that you find really interesting?

If, like many people, your answer is that you haven't had time to develop your interests, but will do it after you retire, please pay attention. 19 You are at high risk of having a difficult—perhaps even miserable—retirement. Few people who have not cultivated authentic interests during their middle years are able to do so after age 65. Many of them end up bored and disappointed.

How long has it been since you've had a genuine new interest or 20 dabbled in an old one? Warning flags should be flying if you are in your 40s or 50s and do not participate in several interesting activities. Put another way, if you do little more than fantasize about what you might do if you had more time or energy after retirement, your fantasies may turn out to be just that.

And keep in mind that hobbies probably won't occupy all your time. 21 Even the most avid fisherman, gardener, traveler, or dog lover is likely to find plenty of time for these activities and many other things as well. After all, will you really be able to—or want to—fill every minute with golf or mah jong?

———————————

Questions About the Reading

1. What percentage of one's life will many Americans live after age sixty-five?
2. What should you do to avoid boredom, and boring others, after you retire?
3. What was the second largest source of income, in 1990, for Americans between sixty-five and seventy-four years of age?
4. What four reasons does the writer give for doing volunteer work?

Thinking Critically

1. What will you do after you retire?
2. What would you do after you retire if you were physically disabled?

Writing Assignments

1. In your journal, list any volunteer work you now do and any hobbies you have.
2. Write an essay explaining how you plan to spend your time during retirement.

Acknowledgments

Chapter 1   Page 4, "Living to Work," from *Unpopular Opinions*, 1946. Reprinted by permission of the Estate of Dorothy Sayers and the Watkins/Loomis Agency; page 6, "In Love With Your Work," by Rhonda Reynolds. Copyright © 1996. Reprinted with permission. *Black Enterprise* magazine. New York, NY. All rights reserved; page 7, "What You Do Is What You Are," by Nickie McWhirter; page 10, "Work and Play," from *Family Album*, by Robert Murray Davis, published by the University of Georgia Press. Reprinted with permission; page 14, "My Mother Never Worked," by Bonnie Smith Yackel, from *Women: A Journal of Liberation*, Vol. 4, #2, 1995; page 19, "Working Just to Live Is Perverted into Living Just to Work," by Ana Vecinana-Suarez. Reprinted with permission of Knight Ridder/Tribune Information Services.

Chapter 2   Page 37, "Choice: Vocation, Career, or Job," by Alan M. Webber. Reprinted from the February/March issue of *Fast Company* magazine. All rights reserved. To subscribe, please call (800) 688-1545; page 41, "Liberal Arts Gave Me a Liberal Dose of Life Lessons," by Rebecca Knight. Copyright © 1998. Reprinted by permission of the author; page 44, "Different Paths to Success," by Joannie M. Schrof. Copyright © 1994, *U.S. News & World Report*; page 48, "Cooperative Education: Learn More, Earn More, Prepare for the Workplace," by Matthew Mariani, from *Occupational Outlook Quarterly*; page 53, "Find Work That You Love," by Barbara Moses. Reprinted with permission of the publisher. From *Career Intelligence*, copyright © 1998 by Barbara Moses, Berrett-Koehler Publishers, Inc., San Francisco, CA. All rights reserved. 1-800-929-2929.

Chapter 3   Page 67, "A Woman's Place," from *We Are Out Mothers' Daughters*, by Cokie Roberts. Copyright © 1998 by Cokie Roberts. Reprinted by permission of HarperCollins Publishers, Inc.; page 73, "Women Who Stay at Home and Love It." Reprinted with permission from *Ebony*, November 1996; page 77, "Being There: The Father Quandary," by Joan K. Peters. Copyright © 1998 by the New York Times Co. Reprinted by permission; page 80, "What Today's Fathers Want," from *Working Fathers* by James A. Levine and Todd L. Pittinsky. Copyright © 1997 by James A. Levine and Todd L. Pittinsky. Reprinted by permission of Perseus Book Publishers, a member of Perseus Books, L.L.C.; page 86, "Still Seeking the Perfect Balance," by Elizabeth McGuire. Copyright © 1998 by the New York Times Co. Reprinted by permission.

Chapter 4   Page 92, "What Is Ethics Anyway?" from *In Pursuit of Ethics* by O.C. Ferrell and Gareth Gardiner, copyright © 1991, Smith Collins Company. Reprinted by permission of the Smith Collins Co.; page 95, "The Twenty Dollar Bill," from "No Advice Here," (pp. 6-7). Appears in *Family Man* by Calvin Trillin. Published by Farrar, Straus & Giroux. Copyright © 1998 by Calvin Trillin. This permission granted by Lescher & Lescher, Ltd.; page 97, "Defining Success," by Michael Korda. Reprinted by permission of International Creative Management, Inc.; page 100, "It's Failure, Not Success," by Ellen Goodman. Copyright © 1979, The Boston Globe Newspaper Co./Washington Post Writer's Group. Reprinted with permission; page 104, "Unethical Workers and Illegal Acts," from *Society Magazine*, May/June, 1999. Reprinted by permission of Transaction Publishers. Copyright © 1999. All rights reserved; page 108, "The Business of Ethics," by John Davidson. First appeared in *Working Woman*, February 1998. Reprinted with the permission of MacDonald Communications Corporation Copyright © 1998 by MacDonald Communications Corporation. www.workingwoman.com. For subscriptions call 1-800-234-9675.

Chapter 5   Page 117, "The Cult of Busyness," from *The Worst Years of Our Lives* by Barbara Ehrenreich. Copyright © 1990 by Barbara Ehrenreich. Reprinted by permission of Pantheon Books, a division of Random House, Inc.; page 121, "Managing Your Time," from *Getting Things Done: The ABC's of Time Management* by Edwin C. Bliss. Condensed with the permission of Scribner, a Division of Simon & Schuster. Copyright © 1976 by Edwin C. Bliss; page 126, "How Not To Lose Friends Over Money," by Lois Duncan, from *Woman's Day*, March 25, 1989, Vol. 49. Copyright © 1989 *Woman's Day*. Reprinted by permission; page 133, "Putting a Lid on Conflicts," by Michael Barrier; page 138, "It's Time to Make up Your Mind," by Winston Fletcher, from *Management Today*, September 1998. Reprinted with permission; page 141, "Truth and Consequences," by Geanne Rosenberg, from *Working Woman*, July/August 1998. Reprinted with permission.

Chapter 6 Page 151, "Women and Physics," by K.C. Kole. Copyright © 1981 by the New York Times Co. Reprinted by permission; page 155, "Do We Need These Laws?" by Andrew Sullivan. Reprinted from *The Advocate,* April 14, 1998. © 1998 by Andrew Sullivan. Used by permission of Liberation Publications, Inc.; page 158, "Earth to Andrew," by Elizabeth Birch. Reprinted from *The Advocate,* May 26, 1998. Reprinted by permission of the Human Rights Campaign; page 161, "Why Black Men Have Lost Ground," by Peter Passell. Copyright © 1991 by the New York Times Co. Reprinted by permission; page 165, "Know Your Rights – And Go For the Job!" by Mary Ann Farrell. Reprinted with permission of Knight Ridder/Tribune Information Services; page 168, "After All This Time, Why Don't People Know What Sexual Harassment Means?" by Anne Fisher. Copyright © 1998 Time, Inc. Reprinted by permission.

Chapter 7 Page 175 – 176, two screen shots from "Career Search jobs," as seen on: www.careermosaic.com. Reprinted with permission; page 178, "The Ins and Outs of E-mail," from *USA Today* Magazine. Reprinted with the permission of The Society for the Advancement of Education; page 181, "Caught in the Net," from *Caught in the Net: How To Recognize the Signs of Internet Addiction – and a Winning Strategy for Recovery* by Kimberly S. Young, copyright © 1998, John Wiley & Sons, Inc. pp. 20-22. Reprinted by permission of John Wiley & Sons, Inc.; page 184, "bigbrother@theoffice.com," by Deborah Branscum. From *Newsweek,* April 27, 1998. Copyright © 1998 Newsweek, Inc. All rights reserved. Reprinted by permission; page 187, "Saying Adios to the Office," by Edward C. Baig. Reprinted from October 12, 1998 issue of *Business Week* by special permission, copyright © 1998 by The McGraw-Hill Companies, Inc.

Chapter 8 Page 194 – 195, sample cover and thank you letters reprinted by permission from the Careermosaic website; page 197, "Set a Course for Lifelong Learning," by Tim O'Brien. Reprinted with permission of Knight Ridder/Tribune Information Services; page 200, "Stop the World, I Want to Get Off," by Cassandra Hayes. Copyright © 1997. Reprinted by permission. *Black Enterprise* Magazine, New York, NY. All rights reserved; page 203, "Traditional Degrees, Nontraditional Jobs: A Degree Is Not a Life Science," by Kathleen Green, from *Occupational Outlook Quarterly*; page 209, "What Will You Do When You Retire?" by Ralph Warner. Copyright © 1999 Nolo.com. Reprinted by permission of Nolo.com.

Index